THE SPIRIT BEHIND THE NEWS

On Finding God in Family, Presidents, Baseball, Cell Phones, and Chevy Impalas

Ben Kamin

I0140412

About Ben Kamin:

"Rabbi Kamin's teachings provide a spiritual lift to anyone who takes up this book."

> *Bishop Anthony M. Pilla*, former president, National Conference of Catholic Bishops

About this book:

"I recognize Ben Kamin's voice—tender, funny, indignant, thoughtful, it's the voice of an ideal pastor, someone whose insights into world events or the even more important trivia of daily life are reliably worth pondering. Reading his reflections on one of recent history's most momentous years, I found myself often agreeing, sometimes dissenting, but always challenged and enlightened."

> *Karl Weber*, co-author (with Muhammad Yunus) of *Creating a World Without Poverty*

Other Books by Rabbi Ben Kamin

Stones in the Soul:
One Day in the Life of An American Rabbi

Raising A Thoughtful Teenager:
A Book of Answers and Values for Parents

Thinking Passover: A Rabbi's Book of Holiday Values

The Path of the Soul:
Making Peace With Mortality

Remora (A novel)

THE SPIRIT BEHIND THE NEWS

On Finding God in Family, Presidents, Baseball,
Cell Phones, and Chevy Impalas

Ben Kamin
Columns, August 2008—January 2009

Muffin Dog Press LLC
Muffindogpress.com

Published by Muffin Dog Press, LLC, PO Box 413, New Windsor, Maryland 21776 USA

Cover art by Brock Denis ©2009
Manufactured by Lightning Source, LaVergne, TN

ISBN: 13: 978-0-9816095-6-0
ISBN: 10: 0-9816095-6-2
Library of Congress Control Number: 2009926155
Religion and spirituality—inspiration
Current events

The text consists mainly of a collection of columns
originally featured on Examiner.com, with minor additional notes.

Please visit the author's website at www.benkamin.com
Please visit the publisher's website at www.muffindogpress.com

Muffin Dog Press, LLC
PO Box 413
New Windsor, Maryland 21776 USA

For Audrey

Acknowledgements

This book is the result of some serendipitous timing of ideas, circumstances, and personalities. A thousand moons ago, Stacie Zoe Berg, now a distinguished business author, was a Hebrew School student of mine in Cincinnati. Much more recently, she urged me join ASJA—the American Society of Journalists and Authors, which led to me a free lance opportunity with "Examiner.com." Through the publication, I befriended fellow Examiner and journalist/editor/ publisher Laura Harrison McBride, who took a liking to the work of this rabbi/commentator valiantly labeled the "Spiritual Life Examiner."

Thankfully, the United States was choosing Barack Obama as its new president during this interval, thereby instigating a host of social, ethical, racial, and even godly issues about which to vent.

Contents

*PLEASE SEE EACH MONTH'S OPENING PAGE FOR A LIST
OF COLUMNS FROM THAT MONTH.*

THE SPIRIT BEHIND THE NEWS

FOREWORD

In August 2008, with the presidential campaign in full velocity, and the country teetering on an economic disaster that would send us reeling (and help ensure the remarkable ascension of Barack Obama to the White House), I was contracted as a columnist by an upstart and ambitious Internet publication called The National *Examiner*. The immediate problem, of course, was to relieve my friends of their concern that this was not <u>the</u> "National Examiner" —a print tabloid of notable and yellow proportions with a penchant for Elizabeth Taylor, Loretta Lynn, Bob Barker, and daytime television.

"No, no," I would caution. "It's 'Examiner.com.' On the web only. A whole new thing, out of Denver."

I am thankful to God Almighty that the National *Examiner* supermarket weekly does not have a web site.

After explaining to them that I was designated as the "Spiritual Life Examiner" and that the column would run nationally, they calmed down. Several of them proactively added their screen names as "Subscribers;" others I simply entered in myself with a certain presumption and attitude. "Oh, is that okay?" I would always ask the person later, upon intersecting at the coffee shop or at a school event with my stepchildren. "Sure, sure," would come the reply. What were they going to say?

In fact, I was in serious and esteemed professional company amidst the roster of "Examiners," including the majority who were manifest in 60 local city editions and the smattering of us known as "national." Many of these experts in cuisine, politics, sports, movies, beer, low-carbohydrate nutrition, computers, automobiles, pets, schools, real estate, atheism, and martinis had come to the cybernetic journal after losing jobs in the print newspaper or magazine industries. You couldn't be a slacker if you were named the "American Idol Examiner" or the "NY Nightlife Examiner." Nor did I have any illusions that a spirituality columnist, though not confined to my denomination and generally able to write about anything that even peripherally hinted at morals or ethics, would ever have anywhere near as many daily "page views" (aka "hits") as the "Miley Cyrus Examiner."

My credentials, happily, were not lacking—nor was my sincere and active desire to be a part of the national discussion during a season of seismic change and indelible memories. Everything was turning on its head in America: racial milestones recalled, social barriers removed, a presidential campaign of eclectic possibilities and unprecedented voter participation and passion.

In August, the Democratic Party nominated Barack Obama for the presidency on the 45th anniversary of Dr. Martin Luther King's "I Have a Dream" preachment on the steps of the Lincoln Memorial. The subsequent inauguration of the nation's first black chief executive followed poignantly just one sunrise after the national celebration of Martin Luther King Day.

Some two million citizens, from innumerable cities, suburbs, hamlets, and farms across the land, appeared on the National Mall in the cold clear sunlight of that January day. The vast majority had no connections to anyone or anything official. They just wanted to be there—close to a surreal moment of history and healing, locking arms with benevolent strangers, sharing tears of relief, joy, disbelief, validation. They sent untold millions of text messages, replete with photos, to their families and friends around the continent, verifying with glee their presence at this rebirth of American hope. My own daughter Sari, our eldest, a New York theater denizen who had been transformed into a vehement politico by the eloquence and intellect of the young senator from Illinois who quietly conquered the Goliaths of Clinton and McCain, dispatched a picture of herself and her boyfriend freezing merrily in the Potomac wind. They felt that they mattered.

Sitting in San Diego warmth in front of my computer at 12 Noon EST that January 20, 2009, watching President Obama pronounce the oath of office spoken only by 42 white men (Grover Cleveland did it twice in nonsuccessive terms) before him, I broke down in tears and attempted to call my other daughter, Debra, a graduate student in Chicago. All circuits were dead; The Moment (as the gods at CNN had dubbed it) ignited an infinite cataclysm of dialing. At the very instant one so vociferously desired,

4

needed, to share this fleeting gleaming breach with someone else, many of us were left in the strange space of aloneness. Then I realized: Better—if you were 56 like me, the son of a churning, interracial, 1960's public high school in Ohio where such a moment had never been conjured up, where bloodshed and assassinations and urban riots and a hemorrhaging war in Vietnam were as much a part of the curriculum as English, geography, and calculus—better to absorb it in the privacy of one's shaking brain chamber and pounding heart.

Other things, some momentous, others not so, and still others just funny, transpired between the August of my immersion into the column and the January transfer of American power.

At first, in the heat of August, finding my voice, I offered a pastoral medley of columns. They were about redemption in the American South (the midsummer humidity always seems to send me back to the South), messiahs, biblical kings who had too many horses, baseball nostalgia, Labor Day and workers' rights, theologies, the September 11 anniversary, and the first of several elegiac recollections of my long-departed and hyper-patriotic immigrant father.

Then, as the two major political parties chose their national tickets of Obama-Biden and McCain-Palin, my meditations and homilies about the democratic system and the landmark ballot became frequent and even acerbic. The political climate yielded gracefully to commemorative associations and cenotaphic declarations; even Senator John McCain could not help but honor the fact that Barack Obama's strapping candidacy came exactly forty years after Dr. King was assassinated. I opined, however, in one righteous column, that the decorated McCain could not claim a moral connection to the civil rights movement, given his original opposition to the creation of a federal MLK holiday. In yet another testament to my concern about the veteran and POW who incongruously chose an inarticulate, rather impetuous novice as his running mate, I pointed out that McCain would become the third consecutive Vietnam combat veteran who lost the presidential election.

Meanwhile, in that quickening autumn, Paul Newman died, the Jewish holidays presented more than one opportunity to reflect on the Jewish roots of Jesus, George W. Bush slipped into obsolescence, the American economy became a matter of bad faith, Elvis continued his national séance, and the

5

devilish president of Iran was invited to address the United Nations General Assembly. All these and other societal symptoms of varied degrees required ruminations from the Spiritual Life Examiner. There was even an opportunity or two to pen public love notes to my wife.

Even as Martin Luther King loomed in so much of the writing (as he has in all my books and Op-ed commentaries for decades), many further topics emerged — some in spiritual tones, all too many in terms of blood and terrorism.

During the bridge between Thanksgiving and Hanukkah, an outlandish terror siege overtook Mumbai, India. Among nearly 200 innocent fatalities of all nationalities, singular and heinous actions were taken against local Jews: The Chabad House, a center of prayer and social services, was seized and its young directors—including a serene, peach-faced rabbi and his wife—were first tortured and then murdered. Their baby survived the spray of bullets and was rescued by an Indian nanny. Like so many, I was gripped and enraged and expressed both the general horror shared with all peoples and the spine-chilling anguish, again, of my own people.

In a blessed coincidence, Hanukkah and Christmas spilled into one another on the calendar, allowing for a dual reflection on shared lights and a recollection of the soaring Apollo 8 Christmas broadcast and prayer to earth from—again—40 years earlier, in 1968. The sanctities and indulgences of not only the holidays, but of media moguls and politicians, especially the presumptively felonious Governor Rod Blagojevich of Illinois, garnered significant notice in a series of "Best Ten" and "Worst Ten" lists. It was, and remains, okay to laugh out loud, even when you are mulling over the spirit.

The end of the year exploded, even while sprinkled with such "Top Ten" flings, with the brutal and inevitable firestorm between Israel and the Hamas terror group ensconced in the desperately wretched Gaza Strip. The conflagration prompted quite a number of painful missives and provoked heated controversy in readers' comments. The conflict took a personal turn as I reported the presence of my own nephew among the Israeli infantry deployed in the fierce little war that was stopped by a ceasefire within hours of the swearing-in of President Barack Hussein Obama.

In this book, 110 of nearly 150 columns, under the aegis of the Spiritual Life Examiner, are reproduced, offering a spiritual diary of the watershed, multifarious, and etched slice of history between mid-August 2008 and the end of January 2009. They deal with everything from the divine authorship

6

of Scripture to the emotional vulnerabilities of a CEO to a lost love at Pearl Harbor to the possible redemption of M.L. King's epochal dream by the electoral college of the United States. Red states, blue states, white skin, black skin, green hopes, and purple hearts all find their way into these compressed expressions of what the rabbinic tradition declared long ago, even as America reinvented itself during these months covered in this book: "God created the world, but people are creating it."

THE SPIRIT BEHIND THE NEWS

On Finding God in Family, Presidents,
Baseball, Cell Phones, and Chevy Impalas

August, 2008

"We human beings are meant to feed the hungry, clothe the naked, and plead for the widowed."

The night fifty college boys lost their voices

August 19, 2008

At the University of Cincinnati, I sang with the men's glee club, mostly classic vocals and many freedom songs inspired by the still lingering memory of Dr. Martin Luther King, Jr. The preacher was gone six years when the club crossed the Mason Dixon line from Cincinnati for a grand tour of the South. Our destination was New Orleans; in between lay a series of performances in auditoriums and church halls from Kentucky to Mississippi. It was 1974, but—as we baritones and tenors were soon to learn—it might as well have been 1934 in such towns as Welch, WVA, and Veramayne, TN.

Arriving one afternoon in the latter community, we were greeted by the local church leaders. It was in their house of worship that we would perform our nightly repertory of show tunes, ballads, and folk songs. Our conductor was always first off the bus. Bill Ermey, thin as a reed, endowed with an iron will that kept our libidos at bay even as our voices were in sync, would make the preliminary arrangements as to set up, equipment checks, and housing.

In this Tennessee borough, however, Bill ran into a little bit of a problem. The town fathers and mothers had peered into the windows of our charter bus and, alas, noticed a sprinkling of black faces among us fifty young men. They gathered into a tight circle of discussion and duplicity as we boys peered out the window. Two or three of them pulled Bill aside, away from the bus, and spoke to him. There would apparently be no houses available for the "Negro boys" to lodge in.

I remember Bill's face as he dragged himself up the steps of the bus. The late afternoon sun emphasized his paleness and pain. "They won't let us all sleep in their homes," he spoke in agony over the static-filled microphone. "Our black members are supposed to spend the night in the motel down the road."

"And they expect us to think of their church as a house of God," called out Larry Tidrow from the rear, already contemplating his career as a Baptist preacher. But his sentiment was being echoed in the throats and hearts of every one of us who sat, stunned, in a Greyhound bus that was now the vehicle of a new and dreadful awareness.

"Well, boys," said Bill now, his voice suddenly strong and thrilled, "I'm your leader. And I say that if we can't all sleep in their houses, then none of us can sing in their church." In the dim light, I saw that Bill's normally pasty face shone with something I had not seen before.

"Well, that's MLK with me!" chimed in the irrepressible Reverend Tidrow.

A burst of cheering and applause rocked the bus, along with a booming cadence of "It's MLK with me!" Bill turned his narrow back around in the doorway, leaned out, and yelled to the nearby cluster of church leaders:

"We're sorry, people, but we will not be singing here tonight. But we do propose that you have a meeting tonight in your church and ask God why these nice boys lost their voices while passing through this town of yours."

The University of Cincinnati Men's Glee Club wound up sleeping aboard the Greyhound that night, parked alongside US 231 in a rather dreary roadside stop that sucked in the darkness. We, however, laughed and sang and eventually slept as cheerfully as our teacher's convictions had been inspired back down the road at a church with no god.

Why do people kill each other?

August 21, 2008

When a youngster asks this question (and certainly many have asked me), the first thing to say is: *Most people don't.*

And yet, it's impossible for any of us not to be thinking about this in an era of media saturation and brazen terrorism. A lot of kids carry a fair amount of anxiety on the subject. Let's face it: Today's youngsters aren't watching grainy serials about "cowboys and Indians." They are routinely watching, on everything from high definition TV sets to YouTube to their own iPhones, clear, immediate video of people of people blowing each other's brains outs.

Here's a perspective: Sadly, this has been going on as long as there have been people living on this planet. It's a fact that people have always hurt one another; the first "recorded" murder involved Cain and Abel of the Bible. Cain didn't pack a handgun, but he did pack human nature. Luckily CNN, Fox, et al weren't around to show the tape a thousand times over and to have a "panel of experts" rehash and review the matter till some of us would be convinced that nothing but fratricide ever occurs in families and neighborhoods—even though most families are basically loving and most neighborhoods are quiet.

We need to remember that there isn't more violence *per capita* in the world than there ever was before. It's just more available for examination. Let's keep this is in mind—while watching over one another, using common sense, and remembering that most people do not kill other people.

Does God favor a candidate?

August 22, 2008

I'm old enough to remember political campaigns that were truly ideologi-
cally driven, passionate, and where a bitter war that seemed—no,
was—hapless and so cruelly unnecessary inspired men and women to debate one another with moral outrage that ultimately favored the soul of
this country. In 1968, for example, my classmates and I were fifteen years
old. We feared the draft, the coiling snake of the Vietnam conflict, and were
terrified every summer that our cities would simply burn down in what
was nothing short of a seasonal race war.

I should think that God is happy that—in spite of everything—we now
have had a woman pioneer pave the way for future female presidents, and
that a black man is about to be formally nominated by a major party for the
presidency. I would imagine that God is happy that, in spite of a spiraling
economy and high gasoline prices, and a glaring list of disparities in America's social structure, we all still enjoy relative peace and calm in the homeland—even as we now burn CDs rather than cities, listen to our iPods
rather than demagogues who preached racism and anti-Semitism routinely
on broadcast networks.

A generation ago, you were cool if you were *liberal* because it meant
that you believed that people are smart enough to think and take comfort
from their faith in deep privacy with God. Now if you are a liberal, you
somehow stand for spineless, social gibberish, weak sympathies for the
poor and uneducated, and you aren't tough enough to deploy young men
and women on military adventures that are dubious at best.

It's not because I'm a Jew that I am deeply concerned about all the
evangelical litmus tests our political candidates are suddenly required to
endure—and their patronizing responses. This country was founded as
God's country exactly because the founders thought that God is secure
enough in His kingdom not to have everybody flail and be self-righteous
and judgmental. Forgive me, but Jesus would sit this one out.

Two people in the same hospital but different gods

Undated

I recently had the occasion to visit two ailing hospital patients and discovered that God is in the perception of the believer. I actually dreaded seeing Mr. Elwood, who was truly suffering the pain of a broken ankle with torn ligaments. Mr. Elwood was exceedingly wealthy and, at the time of my visit, was surrounded by a doting wife and his two adult sons. Known for his grumpiness, a bit unaware of the genuine concern his family had for him, he immediately seized upon my entry into the well-appointed private room: "What kind of God are you selling? I am in so much agony that I'll have to miss the big golf tournament next month! What kind of God would do that to me?"

I listened and nodded and told him that his physical pain was certainly debilitating and that there would surely be other golf tournaments. Then I made my way to see Mrs. Glueck, truly wondering if I had the wherewithal to comfort, now, a person whose spine had been damaged and who was doomed to paralysis.

"Oh, welcome, dear Rabbi!" Mrs. Glueck declared with a big smile, even though she was motionless in a room that was somehow filled with light, although there were no windows. "How are you?" I inquired, immediately drawn to the strange, unlikely sense of *hope* that permeated this very serious situation.

"I am so lucky," said Mrs. Glueck. "The doctors and nurses here are wonderful. People are constantly looking in on me. I have an endless stream of visitors and everyone is so filled with kindness and care. But the best part is my grandchildren. I can't turn my head, of course, but you look at the pictures and drawings they have all done for me. So beautiful. Who can lose hope when you get such love?"

I beheld the simple crayon drawings all about the room, the scrawled declarations of love and prayer, and even as Mrs. Glueck, unable to move, stared at me with a beaming smile, I realized that God was in that hospital room, and that she was even richer than Mr. Elwood had ever been. I also realized that I had work to do—compassionate work—with the man who could win golf tournaments but not much else.

When Bobby Kennedy died, Billy Cole gave away his guns
August 26, 2008

It was sometime that morning in June, 1968, as Robert F. Kennedy died of his gunshot wounds in a Los Angeles hospital, when Billy Cole, a friend and former congregant of mine, made up his mind. He would no longer sell guns in his Jasper, AL discount department store.

The poignant appearance this week of Sen. Edward M. Kennedy at the Democratic Convention brought to mind that summer, exactly forty years ago, when Bobby Kennedy would have surely been nominated for president at the same convention.

Bobby Cole, as successful as he was now shaken in 1968, unquestionably facing a personal dilemma, found his conscience weighing in on his financial accounting: Was it possible that any of the firearms he routinely sold had been used to kill someone, as Sirhan Sirhan had just murdered Senator Kennedy, or James Earl Ray had gunned down Rev. Martin Luther King, Jr. just eight weeks earlier in that blood-drenched American year of 1968?

Forty years ago, we were also embroiled in a presidential campaign scorched by racism and an incomprehensible war.

Cole, an Auburn football alumnus who rarely left the magnolias, camellias, and pines of north central Alabama, wanted to follow his scruples quietly and without fanfare. But the media, sensing a real story of hope in a time of trepidation, pursued him. His transfer of $20,000 worth of guns and pistols to Captain Terrence Williams of the Birmingham Police Department was broadcast on NBC's Huntley-Brinkley Report. Cole, an affluent, bourbon-drinking, good-natured man who gambled with celebrities in Las Vegas, also appeared on the national news program but was self-effacing and reluctant to create a fuss about himself.

"I couldn't stand it anymore," he declared. "I had to do something that was more important than the bottom line."

A wide spectrum of publications cited the owner's decision, including *Newsweek, Time,* and *Business Week.* An unpublished—but even more important—document was the family scrapbook put together by Cole and his brother Nate, who was the other partner at Cole's Department Store. It was necessary because an endless flow of letters began in the aftermath of the businessman's decision. Many congratulated him and shared harrowing but inspirational memories—crucibles of terror and helplessness that Cole's action released and help heal.

From Boston—"Dear Sir: More power to you. I lost a son at 18 by a gun, unnecessarily. Good luck."

From Phoenix—"My sister's husband went into a drugstore and bought a gun, then waited for their children to come home and killed them, one by one. He then waited for my sister Mitzi and killed her and then late that night, he killed himself. Mr. Cole, thank you again."

Such notes and such stories filled the fading scrapbook, although the decision Cole made also invited not-so-friendly messages:

"Because you did retire as trash-gun merchant with much trumpeting on behalf of the Socialist-Communist Crusade to disarm the American populace, you have lost one customer."

"Now Mr. Cole, it seems that you and your little brother may be of Jewish descent...

"I bought from you when you were in a tent but I shall never buy another item from you because of your cheap stand on guns."

The fact is that after Billy Cole's fateful decision in the summer of 1968, a choice made in favor of moral currency, sales at his department store began a precipitous decline. The store finally shut down in the early 1970s. Nate Cole, unable to bear all the criticism and bitter about his economic losses, left Alabama and resettled in Florida. He rarely spoke to Billy anymore. But Billy went on to other enterprises and remained a person of cheerful good spirits for the remainder of his years. He finished with considerably less wealth than he had in 1968. But he told me that he felt like a rich man and that he was prepared for the outcome of the cardiovascular ailments that finally took him in 1997. He was a man at peace who mentioned to me more than once: "About giving away the guns, I was never happier than with any other decision I made." It was clear that Billy Cole learned a lot about himself in that momentous choice.

Bobby, you didn't die in vain, even as one man heard more than the gunfire.

Dr. King would have voted for this
August 27, 2008

Whatever your politics, it's hard not to note that Sen. Barack Obama's acceptance of the Democratic nomination for president exactly coincides with the 45th anniversary of Rev. Martin Luther King's "I Have A Dream" speech and vision. Whatever your politics, this has to raise one's spirits as an American. To my stepchildren, in their teens during this historic confluence of history, race, and dreams, there is no discernible race issue. They understand and honor the jubilation people such as me feel in the meaning of Obama's milestone candidacy but, to everyone's benefit, they don't quite realize what the big deal was. In that polite default of theirs is a fulfillment of Dr. King's words at the Lincoln Memorial on August 28, 1963: "I have a dream—that one day my children will be judged not by the color of their skin, but by the content of their character."

My step kids in 2008 are sending text messages and interfacing on MySpace with black kids, Asian, Muslim, Jewish, Latino—they have no rainbow, just the sky itself. My own daughters, politically active and in their 20's, feel the trembling excitement of walking across a previously forbidden bridge.

It is not all harmony, and it never will be. What started in the Bible, that is, human prejudice and the proclivity to violence, will never end. There is still a beastly war to protest, 40 years after Vietnam. Nooses have appeared on college campuses and in city squares—a most grisly reminder of the deepest Southern tradition of racial contempt. The economic gap in America remains an indictment of America's fairness doctrine, and it cuts across racial lines.

An elderly Martin Luther King Jr. likely would have spoken and written about this postmodern version of national discrimination. He would have only been 79 this year and would have called us to distinguish between the security of our border and our plain old insecurity about brown immigrants.

He certainly would have smiled at Barack Obama; the thunder and lightning that made him wince at the Masonic Temple in Memphis on the night of April 3, 1968—when he eerily prophesied his own death that occurred the next evening—would have given way to some fresh light and happy noise.

Forty-five years after The March, Dr. King would nonetheless be most jubilant that we all have the right to vote, and that whatever our politics, we all can cast our dreams.

First plant the tree...
August 28, 2008

A lot of folks seem very certain about God these days. A millennia-old tradition from rabbinic sages suggests that's not necessarily the best way to go. Believing in God is wonderful and elating; depending on God, or swearing God's reliability can bring good people some real heartache.

We are God's partners; it's not for us to sit by and let God clean up our messes, create social justice, or decide our elections. We human beings are meant to feed the hungry, clothe the naked, and plead for the widowed. Manna doesn't come down from the sky anymore; it's processed in hunger centers and food cooperatives and in the hearts of people who are inspired by God.

If the doers of good works stood by and waited for God to deliver the goods, well, we'd have more self-righteousness and a lot of empty bellies. Right-wing Jews, Christian evangelicals, and Islamic fundamentalists—who co-opt God in ways that surely bring tears to the heavenly angels—might learn from an old tale found in the Talmudic literature.

A person asked a rabbi, "If I'm planting a tree, and someone comes along and announces that the Messiah has arrived, what shall I do?" The rabbi's response: "First finish planting the tree; it's more of a sure thing."

Labor Day: Work, children, and the spirit

August 30, 2008

On this summer-ending holiday that exalts labor, it is good to consider that work is a gift in and by itself. What working or volunteering actually do for the human spirit is lost in the rush of Labor Day shopping excursions, backyard picnics, and swimming pool closings. We parents would plead for a national day of reflection on the power and redemption of work—especially as it applies to our children. This would be especially valuable as families contemplate the pending anniversary of the September 11 attacks.

Many American children have a lot, but they feel little. We supply them an endless cornucopia of stuff but we don't necessarily allow them the fruits of their own labor. They have a wealth of information, but they are depleted in experience. It is a fair guess that a significant portion of teenagers don't even know that Labor Day is a uniquely western festival having to do with the advent of labor unions and workers' rights. While Labor Day was invented to protect wages, labor itself protects people from listlessness. Many educators believe that meaningful and appropriate labor can also be transforming for children.

Ask most any schoolteacher or guidance counselor: In order to feel good about themselves, children must toil or complete a creative project on their own. Being handed material things, empty flattery, or patronizing remarks about their looks or background do not create lasting self-esteem. Doing productive work that is dignified and fair does.

An irony: We parents have never been working harder. We venerate work, are driven by work, and allow work to even contravene quality family time. Yet we are afraid of work for our children. We give them the material benefits of our own productivity, but deny them the spiritual benefits of producing things for themselves.

Human beings, including children, need to engage in meaningful work that asks all of us to sacrifice something and not just gain a paycheck. There are internal rewards that do not turn up on evaluation forms or salary statements. These are increments to the soul that, if not learned by children every day, will continue to make Labor Day just another day.

September, 2008

Scripture's language is rustic, perhaps, but telling nonetheless:
A king shall not have too many horses.

"People make plans and God laughs"
September 1, 2008

This is not a political column in any way—other than in the reality that even politicians dabble in faith, pursue or lasso God, and fear mortality. As these words are written on Monday morning, September 1, millions of Americans have fled from deathly winds and rising waters along the Gulf Coast. So eerily, but even more urgently, Gustav rains down upon Louisiana and Mississippi and nearby parts—three years exactly from the murderous landfall of Katrina in 2005.

We are grateful, at this writing, that, evidently, so many children and adults and pets have evacuated to safer grounds in anticipation of the storm. We pray that their homes will be spared and—even as so many still suffer from the shock of Katrina and the governmental failures that exacerbated that debacle—they themselves will resume a certain normalcy and hopefulness again soon. We plead in our hearts that no city will drown again, that levees will stay the waters, that people will do their jobs for the simple purpose of saving lives and sparing suffering and not because it favored the public relations of this party or that.

An old Yiddish aphorism: "People make plans, and God laughs." The organizers of the 2008 Republican National Convention, about to launch their candidates, their platforms, and their special effects (just as the Democrats did one week ago), found themselves living this bit of raw theology.

It is, frankly, hard not to extract some level of political expediency from their initial suspension of the festivities in deference to what nature was dealing our Gulf Coast. History—and a scalding failure—stared them in the face.

These notes are dedicated to the hope that the good citizens of the area come through this terrifying event okay and that the belief that even politicians caught their breath in our ultimate obeisance to something larger than a big speech.

A king shall not have too many horses
September 3, 2008

In this heady time of national decision, the Old Scripture unhesitatingly calls for appropriate restraints on any king. It's fair to say that the notion of "limited government" and "checks and balances" are not recent manifestations; they're actually 3,000 years old and come straight out of Deuteronomy and, hopefully, directly into the Democratic and Republican platforms of 2008.

There is recognition in the early Bible that the Israelites would want to anoint a king, once they had settled in Israel and established themselves among the family of nations. Now, a king is not necessarily the same thing as a president or a prime minister. But the intent is the same: To establish a leader who is able to lead but not lose touch with the people led. Scripture's language is rustic, perhaps, but telling nonetheless: *A king shall not have too many horses.*

Every September, when I come to this eye-lifting admonition in the Jewish cycle of Scriptural readings—but especially in this election year—I'm struck by its old-fashioned insight. A ruler with too many horses, or limousines, or airplanes, is a ruler at risk of losing touch. I'm amazed by how much old wisdom and pragmatism is packed into this unlikely declaration about powerful men (and women) and realism. I'm hoping that the increasingly vocal and theologically righteous segment of our national political management is actually reading some lesser-known parts of the Bible.

Those holy-toting folks (of all parties) who politicize the electoral process of this good nation might want to read a couple of verses beyond the warning about the king with too many horses. The king is also warned "not to take too many wives for himself." But not only that: The king is directed "not to take too much gold and silver for himself" and to keep not one, but *two* copies of Scripture around the palace.

This is the kind of Bible I'll take with me to the ballot box.

Arab and Jew, we were just two boys under the orange trees
September 6, 2008

The cyclical carnage from Palestinian suicide bombings and Israeli retaliations make it hard to believe that peace in the Holy Land is possible. Yet each outrage, followed by unending grief and fierce response, makes me think even more about a little dialogue I had long ago with a Palestinian neighbor of mine.

Every now and then I read about the Palestinian town of Qalqilya and terrorists who might be seeking shelter there. But Qalqilya is not just a passing news reference for me.

In the fall of 1961, I was eight years old and living in the Israeli hamlet of Kfar Saba, where my parents had also been born. We could see the Samarian Mountains from our porch, and the town of Qalqilya, then part of Jordan, with its minarets and stone streets, just a mile or so away. A valley of orchards and wild brush hung between us and was forbidden; the border was more or less defined by an old rail path left behind by the British, who had quit their mandate in Palestine five years before I was born.

But exactly because the citrus-scented valley between Kfar Saba and Qalqilya was off limits to us, it was enticing to me one Saturday afternoon that fall. I rode my bicycle past the village square, beyond the old bus station, and into the valley that unfolded against the biblical mountains. Qalqilya was close by where I walked in the thick groves that divided the two worlds. And then I realized that I was not alone. Standing by and staring at me was an Arab boy, about my age, as surprised by this encounter as I.

We both froze in fear. But curiosity quickly prevailed and we began to talk. It was a halting mixture of Hebrew and English; I did not know any Arabic. I still remember that he knew words from both of my languages and I did not know any from his. And I still remember his face very clearly, particularly the way that he smiled.

I told him about my village and described my father as a war hero and a mighty man who had once fought in that valley. He told me that his father was very tall and strong and was chieftain of his village. We talked about the orange trees and agreed to meet again in a week at the same spot. I told him my name. He told me his—Ahmed. We parted, the sons of fathers who may have battled each other in that valley.

Our second appointed meeting was washed out by an autumn rain, but we did again meet several days later. I had not told my parents about the first meeting because they would certainly have disapproved. Ahmed stood waiting for me. We barely touched shoulders. There was a tension we did not understand. But we were driven by something very good that we also did not understand.

We both knew that this second meeting would confirm the first but necessarily be the last. Nevertheless, it was truly friendly. We taught each other words from each other's languages, simple words like "goat," "bicycle" and "rain." We compared notes on siblings. And then the time grew short. Before leaving, we did something together, reaching almost simultaneously for the same large orange hanging down from the tree above us, we opened it and shared the slices. How sticky and sweet it tasted. We buried the peels and the seeds in the ground under the tree. And we promised to meet at the spot again one day, the day when peace came between our people.

I remember Ahmed's face. In the television footage of rage coming to us from that same valley, I look for that face. We are both middle-aged men now and, on a recent visit, I saw that few trees were left in that valley. Israeli tanks have had to roll into Qalqilya across the years. Unforgivable bombings have killed children in my birth village. I wonder where Ahmed is and what we would say to each other if we were to meet again. Might it be possible for us reach a reconciliation now? Would he remember that we once knew more about peace than all of the grown-ups on either side of our valley?

This essay originally appeared in *The New York Times.*

Religion is science with love
September 8, 2008

The Bible never tells us what exactly is meant by "Six Days of Creation." There is no description of clockwork or twenty-four hour days; six
days could have been six million units of time that have nothing to do with
the digital timer in everybody's bedroom.

Therefore, and particularly at this time of heated religious righteousness, let me say that evolution is entirely compatible with the Book of Genesis.

Meanwhile, religion, from Zen to Catholicism, is basically a flight from
loneliness. The Babylonians who watched the Milky Way, the Egyptians
who envisioned divine nostrils, the Hebrews who chanted prayers according to the rhythm of the harvest seasons, all craved the presence of gentle-
ness and friendship in the mystery that was bigger than they.

All of these people, in various degrees, wrote significant astrological
charts, devised numerologies, built bridges, and charted the oceans. But
none of them, even the scientific Platonists of Greece, could comprehend
existence without the hand of God.

They all pursued science, even as we in the twenty-first century continue to master it in many ways. But we also look for spirituality in so
many ways. So, let us agree that religion is science with love.

When my daughter introduced God to me
September 9, 2008

One evening at home, some time ago, I was feeling sorry for myself. Alone in the house, I let the demons get the better of me. Things were not going so well at work; I was uncertain about my efforts and despondent in general. I stared out the kitchen window into the rain-washed garden and saw nothing but myself.

For several days, I hadn't let anybody in my family help me. Now, as I gazed out into the backyard, the family car pulled in. I withdrew even more in self-pity. Suddenly my younger daughter Debra, then about twelve, burst into the room, oblivious to my mood, smiling and excited. She had just returned from a family shopping excursion and had something to share: "Dad, *guess* what we saw?!

I barely responded, though something in her spirit lifted my eyes. My daughter continued: "Oh my! You should have seen it! It was a rainbow in the sky, Dad. A double rainbow! Oh, it was *so beautiful*! All of a sudden, Dad, there it was—a rainbow!"

I looked up, as Debra's thrilling words broke through my loneliness with light, color, and hope. I realized that God was speaking to me through my child. When does God talk to us? When another person comes along to make the sound.

Sept. 11 and the ache in our soul
September 11, 2008

It was not a crusade or a mission that brought me to New York City on a prior anniversary of September 11. It was a visit with my adult daughters, who are also going to vote this November, and who are patient with my unyielding, moldy-fig reflections on a dear nation that has neither crusade nor mission in the air. But, on a surprisingly balmy day, with constant glances at the date box on my watch, I thought I saw, heard, and even voted in the national spiritual poll that has more to do with consolation than contention.

As I gazed down Sixth Avenue on that September 11, 2004, the glaring absence of the two towers on the horizon spoke to me more than anything the presidential candidates of that year had to say.

Still today, there is a hole in our national soul. We look for people on the national ballot who seem to have sensitivity to our true pathos, candidates who reveal bit of poetry and reflection. Too often, they are accusatory rather than elegiac; some exchange war yarns for the sake of advantage rather than honest patriotism, they rely on slogans and they stand around sometimes puffy firefighters rather than asking us any good questions or standing for the children of fighters, teachers, doctors, technicians, or a host of non-comic book or poll-boosting post-9/11 quasi-icons.

Though they protest, candidates sometimes don't seem to know anything about us; it's an unsettling mix of strangers vying for the digital loyalty of more strangers—meaningless flares of 'lipstick' and 'earmarks.'

I was nonetheless lifted and touched by my walks with my daughters through the day and evening of that September 11 in New York. There was festive music in the air as bands and choirs gathered in the parks and sang songs that were somberly joyous. Break dancers performed for delighted plebeian circles of folks whose faces and eyes and lips filled the circles with delicious colors and creeds. No one was scared, just as no one was really electrified politically. Liturgies hung over the city and across the quietly grieving sky that looked like an atmospheric scar. Yet there was no sadness, really—just plenty of meaning, caring, and quiet defiance. The vote was being cast—in favor of the American spirit. You just didn't feel that the actual candidates were anywhere near the polls. Perhaps this election will yet lift that spirit.

My father blended the rose petals with the thorns
September 12, 2008

Whenever I perform the funeral service for somebody's father, I think, naturally, of my own father's death, much too young, well over thirty years ago.

I know that my father apprehended his death. I discovered evidence of this in his journals, which I read sometime after his sudden demise—from a massive heart attack. In painful, searching prose, my father inscribed his struggle with himself in the months before his inglorious end. A mild heart attack two years earlier not only failed to help him discern life better, it actually provoked his proud and vain spirit.

He could not give in to the reality of his vulnerability, dismissing the precaution and care prescribed by his physicians and pleaded for by his anxious family. He had been an award-winning athlete in college; he was a physically strong and virile young man who made something of a name for himself in his adopted America. A scientific engineer, he participated in some of the designs related to the Gemini space program, including the heat shield for the renowned two-man starship.

He seemed, in his agonizing diaries, to both defy and dread his sentence of mortality. On one hand, he complained of the restrictions to his physical activity that his heart condition imposed. On the other hand, he prophesied that he could see himself in a coffin at the local funeral home. My father was a good man at war with himself, and, ironically, I have learned more from his death than his life.

And this is okay, because as autumn approaches, and the leaves change, and we think of our beloved dead, it doesn't matter how they taught us. My father, always fragrant with his hallmark aftershave, blooming with immigrant idealism, was like a rose, blending petals with thorns. My father, given to bursts of sentiment, short on patience, never wore a crown of willows.

Baseball is memory; it's in the blood
September 13, 2008

Arlin Schumann may not have liked the postmodern ambiance of today's retro baseball parks, but they sure would have liked his grumpy fan credentials. Any place where the game is played, and fans cheer, and ball counts are maintained, would have welcomed this curmudgeon of a genuine ballyard creature. In fact, his life depended on it.

If Arlin Schumann had known about steroids and human growth hormones, he still would have grumbled joyously about the vicissitudes of the game that kept him alive through much of another afflicted baseball season. Baseball has a way of transcending even baseball players, a rhythm and cadence that ensures its survival even when some are out at home. The current troubles, the hearings, the taint and the heartache, send me back to a man who was attached to both kidney machines and box scores. I visited him frequently as both he and baseball struggled to breathe, in 1981, and think of him in the summer baseball breezes.

Arlin Schumann, in his late 50s, laid up, was nevertheless spirited and chatty. He measured the flow of his dialysis treatments in a Long Island facility as against the fluctuations of the baseball standings. While visiting my friend, I discovered his built-in sense of the present and future by his daily measurement of "where they stand." His face drained of color, his eyes still shining, he took stock of the world he clung to by his regular declaration: "All right. I've gotta check the baseball."

But that summer, the ballplayers went on strike, and the standings stalled. A horrible inertia permeated the sports pages of Arlin's *Newsday*. Midseason, the critical cycle of wins and losses, of stats and streaks, simply stopped like a deadened summer breeze. The pumped blood still flowed through Arlin's machine, cleansed and life-sustaining, but it seemed to fade further from the fullness of his cheeks. Some 50 games vanished from the schedule, 50 units of time, space, and order for this downcast fan who could no longer "check the baseball."

He told me, "I don't get stuck on any of the players too much. It's the game that matters. That's going to go on, no matter what any bum may do." I think Arlin might have gone easy on Roger Clemens, in the end. He might have even forgiven Barry Bonds.

So, short on games, Arlin began to tell me about a visit he made twenty years earlier to the Baseball Hall of Fame in Cooperstown, NY. "Kennedy was president," he remembered, "and the Yanks clobbered the Reds, 4-1, in the World Series." He sighed, letting out pain and shaking off the indignity of his infirmity with the therapy of memory.

Arlin spoke of Cooperstown and its shining Otsego Lake, a long oval mirror edging along state route 80, widening its mouth near the baseball village. He described the wooded mountain grounds of the region, tucked far enough away from the New York Thruway to retain their freshness and their scented seclusion. His baseball story, joining him in his fight for life, fueled his mind, and
saved the game from itself.

There in that sterile hospital cubicle, I could see the lake near Doubleday Field. I could traverse the rich cattle pastures and thick cornfields along the two-lane highway. I could smell the apple trees and the wildflowers of the baseball valley.

When something in baseball saddens me, I remember the testimony of my private knothole laureate. I angle across Otsego Lake, past Glimmerglass State Park, and on through Kingfisher Tower, Natty Bumppo's Cave, and Fairy Springs Park. Baseball is not an injunction, it is a narrative. Baseball cleanses itself; I understood that from the oral tradition of my nostalgic friend who dreamed again of boating the Susquehanna River, docking at the Springfield Public Landing, and walking through Main Street to check out Hank Aaron's 715th home run ball in the Hall of Fame.

"When you get there next," Arlin told me, "make sure to show your kids Babe Ruth's locker. It's the actual locker from Yankee Stadium." Indeed, as I saw a few years later with my daughters, the Locker, like an archaeological relic, stands in the center of the hall, surrounded by trophies, uniforms, bats, and other mementos of "No. 3."

Along the edges of the exhibits, the chronicles of a solar game not stopped by a clock or a penalty, a game whose coordinates are measured not in yards but in yarns, an enterprise so knowing that a man's constant goal is to simply come home—or offer himself as a sacrifice—were being woven and rewoven by fathers and children, by mothers and grandfathers. Cheerful guides in shiny red blazers directed us to famous baseballs and eternal plaques. If only Arlin was there, I think to myself, how dashing he'd be in one of those sport coats, his pulse maintained by runs, bases, hits, and "where they stand."

It's the game itself that fills our summers. Baseball, I once saw for myself, is in the blood. Baseball is memory.

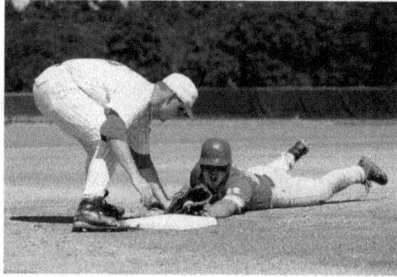

We come and go from this world unadorned
September 15, 2008

The rabbi, though mortally afflicted with sarcoma, nonetheless held fast to his title and credentials. He didn't like it when people failed to use his title, 'Rabbi,' in any discourse—especially in public. He came from a long line of rabbis and, in fact, had ascended to his senior position at a prominent and historic temple upon the death of his very famous rabbi-father. There was almost a royal lineage associated with the family; this Ph. D.-rabbi had never really worried about money, status, and had never actually gone through the rigors of applying for a job. He had inherited it—though he absolutely dignified his position for over thirty years with distinguished service and world-class scholarship.

I liked him, and was his junior on the staff. We had an affectionate relationship and a good understanding: He didn't pretend to be a populist and instead produced extraordinary and well-crafted weekly sermons and published books of academic distinction. He let me be the "people person," the one who mingled with the children and was folksy and humorous while he led—effectively—from a distance.

I liked him enough to mistakenly refer to him by his first name during one of the temple's annual meetings. He fumed afterwards and admonished me: "Don't you ever call me 'Bob' in front of the congregation. To you, I'm Rabbi Robert Roth, and that's it."

But when Rabbi Roth (not his real name) contracted a devastating brain cancer at the much too young age of 59, his pedigree began to matter less and his humanity much more. We could not have not have been more dissimilar, yet converged along a symmetry that made things work and surely made working with him for those two final years poignant and visceral.

One afternoon, I assisted him and his wife as he underwent yet another series of treatments at the local clinic. We three languished unhappily in the crowded waiting lobby. His hair was gone, and his strapping good looks, but not his dignity. Yet: When it was the rabbi's turn to be called to the treatment room, the indifferent receptionist called out: "Mr. Roth?"

In God's plan, titles and accolades mean nothing; we come and go from this world unadorned.

So now they are angels; they wanted to be women
September 16, 2009

Simply because they were black, and defenseless, four little girls were blown up in their church forty-five years ago, September 15, 1963. In an era of significant social milestones, when a black man is the presidential nominee of one of our two major parties, this date is a national scar on the calendar of American civil progress and spiritual growth.

Monday was the anniversary of the ghoulish bombing of Birmingham's 16th Street Baptist Church—an original act of terrorism perpetrated by Americans against Americans. Just three weeks after Dr. Martin Luther King's immortal *I Have A Dream* preachment in Washington, DC, members of the Ku Klux Klan planted nineteen sticks of time-release dynamite in the basement of one of Alabama's most venerable houses of God.

Their names were Denise McNair, Cynthia Wesley, Carole Robertson, and Addie Mae Collins. The dynamite had been planted by the Klansmen specifically under the corner of the church where these children would be donning their white robes for Sunday choir. Denise was 11 years old, the other three were 14. Their interests ranged from sewing to reading to softball to Girl Scouting. Denise was friends at the time with the future Secretary of State, Condoleezza Rice. Another 22 people were injured in the brutal explosion that sprayed stained glass, pews, prayer books, blood, and hope across 16th Street and the heart of our nation.

Dr. King came to eulogize the little girls as well as innocence itself: All they were guilty of, declared the shaken preacher, was a yearning for love.

Two more black teenagers were killed in the aftermath of the bombing. Johnny Robinson and Virgil Ware were shot wantonly in separate incidents, one by police, and one by white passersby.

The sad scroll of Birmingham's little girls is creased with some relief: Strangers of all colors spontaneously visited the mourning houses of their parents. Eight thousand mourners attended the funeral, which was co-officiated by clergymen of three denominations. President Kennedy, who had initially opposed the March on Washington for political reasons, now began to talk about an historic civil rights bill which, ironically, would be enacted after the president's own murder—in 1964.

The four little girls are angels, when they would have preferred to be women today. If we forget them, then we will forget our national soul.

I lost my friend along the way
September 17, 2008

Jack Bluestein was my classmate and my cohort in graduate school; we studied together to become rabbis. Heavy-shouldered, overachieving, and wickedly funny, Jack had played football in college, married too young, and, as it turned out, chose the rabbinate because he sought to become the first Jewish television evangelist. I actually never quite accepted Jack's rather self-serving view of the clergy, and his uproarious personal habits sometimes made me nervous, but I recognized immense talent coming from his busy brow.

We were inseparable during those formative years, studying for exams together through the nights, playing pranks on our classmates during the days, fielding a school softball club together, devouring life at a time when it seemed as eternal as it was demanding. My friend was ravenous…for recognition, for acceptance, for emotional gratification, for late-night repasts, for a piece of the sky. Although I knew of his vanity, I was constantly drawn to him for his insightful and devastating humor, his ability to win people over, and his utter brilliance.

When, years later, I suddenly found myself watching Jack Bluestein on CNN's *Larry King Live* discussing his new-wave, big-tent Jewish "revival," I knew that my friend was in the full throttle of his robust ambition. I laughed out loud, recalling the time he had literally placed rubber-tipped toothpicks in his eyes to tell me that he was going to be up all night to study for a Talmud exam.

What I did not know when I discovered Jack on network television was that he was already a leukemia patient. After graduating together, he had gone down to Florida to start a congregation, and I went to Canada for my first posting. Freed of academic pressures, we no longer needed each other in the same way. He would call me on the telephone once in a while, make me laugh, and then go out and get himself some more airtime somewhere. His tenuous marriage finally foundered. But, as it turns out, he was sick; his mighty torso was weakening from poor blood counts, marrow transplants, and chemotherapy. He mentioned his ailment to me from time to time but I refused to imagine him as anything but hale and boisterous.

I had seen Jack during a visit to Florida just prior to the diagnosis. It had been a good sojourn; he confided things to me about his professional goals, his romantic life, and his disdain for organized religion. The other rabbis in his community shunned and disliked him. Although his lifestyle made me uncomfortable, I found a strange bit of truth in his vision of Judaism without walls, and thought that he was the one who could and should pursue it.

All in all, however, I gave Jack a cursory place in my mind. I went on with my career and basically lost track of him—until the Larry King appearance. We saw each other one more time during a rabbinic convention. He told me that he was going to overcome "this cancer thing" and still had big plans. "My congregation renewed my contract," he declared, sounding like a veteran football player who had been given a sentimental extension. He looked small, nervous, lonely. It occurred to me that somebody like Jack could actually die. I didn't think that somebody like *me* could die; but that Jack maybe could.

He called my office, now in Cleveland, many months later. My secretary told me that he was funny, but really sounded troubled. "He wants to talk to you." I wrote myself a note to call Jack sometime.

The note was still in a file in my desk when the newsletter published by our rabbinical conference arrived about a month later. As everybody who gets such a professional newsletter invariably does, I turned almost immediately to the personal items. There, under the obituary announcements, I read the name JACK BLUESTEIN. I reached for my forehead in panic and shock. I looked at the name again, literally rubbing my eyes. I checked the other three names in that month's column. Their lifespans made more sense: 79 years old, 82 years old, 91 years old. Under Jack's name, the announcement read "1950-1990," and "Survived by his Parents and Children."

Salty water running down my cheeks, I reached into the desk file. I pulled out the note I had made myself just weeks earlier. I stared at the telephone and put my head down in remorse, despair, and not a little bit of trembling. "Oh, Jack!" I heard myself cry out in the hollowness of my study.

The next day, I wrote an anguished note to Jack's parents. They surely would remember me; after all, Jack and I had been close buddies, and he had served as an usher at my first wedding. I recalled that when my father died just months after the wedding, Jack didn't leave my side for days. "I can hear Jack's laughter right now," I wrote to his mom and dad. I never received a reply from the parents of the friend I had presumed.

Jack was not a saint. I'm not even certain that he was a perfect father or an effective rabbi. But Jack was mortal, and this is the part I neglected shamelessly. His death, bereft of my good-bye or even my acknowledgment, has serviced my intention to regard human life and human mortality with a reverence equal to the emptiness I knew the day I read his name in somebody else's journal.

My beautiful and tired America needs inspiration
September 18, 2008

In Barcelona recently, I asked a general store clerk for postage stamps; there were postcards to mail home to California and Ohio. "I don't have stamps for America," he responded contemptuously, standing in front of a full display case of stamps. "But I see stamps there," I barked. He glared: "I have stamps, yes, but not for America." I took my business elsewhere, my heart pounding with dismay.

"The nation is falling apart," some say. "Things aren't what they used to be," others sigh. You've been hearing it and, likely, you've been uttering it. Without question, we are being tested, and from the point of our relative experience, we citizens are run down. Sorry, but there isn't that much consolation for the working parent, trying to fuel up the family car at well over $4.00 a gallon, in being told that folks are paying $9.00 for it in Madrid.

Our spirits are down and it is understandable. We were raised to believe in America's special condition, its unique destiny, and in its exemplary role as a liberty model. This was covenantal, and it was indoctrinated by school textbooks and presidential proclamations.

My beautiful and tired America is looking for inspiration—and relief from doldrums that range from the pocketbook to our reputation. Many of the responses we are getting (notwithstanding the increasingly spiteful cycle of the presidential contest) are too extreme to be borne by the grandmothers of St. Louis, the dock haulers of Boston, the shift workers of Detroit, the school kids of Colorado Springs, the teachers of Los Angeles, the bus drivers of Portland, the farmers of Montana. On one hand, we are told to simply "turn off"—a chilling notion. On the other hand, we are admonished to be "saved"—a hyper-religious alternative that may soothe the psyche but doesn't reconfigure anybody's debt, mortgage, or college loan burdens.

An uncommon teenager named Anne Frank wrote in her diary, "In spite of everything, I still believe that people are good." The fourteen year-old had bigger problems than most any of us, hiding from the Nazis in an Amsterdam attic with her family. The optimistic child would perish in

Auschwitz, but her faith in human resiliency is as immortal as the human spirit.

Here in the United States, a brimming nation of over 300 million people, most of whom are very good and well-intended, we do have problems to solve and images to repair—along with our schools, freeways, bridges, and perhaps even the electoral system. But regardless of who leads us, and how well they do, it's still *our* country, and the overwhelming majority of us still just wants to buy groceries in peace, get to school, be creative at work, and believe again that our kids will do better than us. Let our leaders follow our example of moderation, hard work, reasonable faith expectations, and generally good spirits that have always been the hallmarks of those of us not making a lot of noise.

While two vowed love, two others spoke hate
September 22, 2008

Yesterday, as I performed a wedding and the couple rejoiced, two other people cursed me and my children. Sunlit skies and delicious temperatures along San Diego's downtown coast failed to soften the hearts of those who disdain love and co-opt merciful God.

The groom, a former Marine, hails from Indiana, and a childhood of personal tumbleweed, family upheaval, and angry relationships. His roots are in Christianity but his heart was leavened by a diminutive, firm-willed, crystal-eyed Jewess from Montreal. My sense—and my professional discipline now for several years—is that God is happy when two people find peace and union, and the ability to hope, even when they came from different places to meet under a canopy. God knows this world is already in enough trouble in the category of religious righteousness.

Jason and Marissa worked hard for their marriage to come true and they freely chose a rabbi, working alone, to bless them and turn their divergent paths into one. They were inspired by the prophet Amos, who once asked, "Can two walk together, unless they have agreed?" They studied Moses, whose first and enduring love was for Zipporah—a woman of 'pagan' origins, whose father was hardly Jewish (in fact, he was a Midianite priest!) and who nonetheless became Moses' most tender advisor and supportive Dad. Just read the Bible.

The bride and groom, in their commitment to one another, their well-considered struggles with the "religious questions," did more work on this issue, and the issues of children, spirituality, and authenticity, than most well-meaning couples who simply walk down the aisle of life.

That's why I was not disheartened by the fervent Baptist present who asked me, prior to the ceremony, as the harpist played and the breeze forgave, if my own children had ever been baptized? Well, no, I responded, it wouldn't have been part of the plan. "Then you know, of course, that they will burn in hell."

Nor was I dismayed when the Orthodox Jew, visiting from Toronto, declared that I am "a fraud" because I would perform "such a wedding" and thereby defile the Torah. I didn't respond, thinking about how often the Torah pleads for understanding, and cries out against intolerance.

The Jews call the wedding canopy "a little sanctuary," and therein I heard God as two human beings pledged to respect one another just as Adam and Eve had done in their own garden. I still believe that God was the gardener.

They'd rather be bathing in the sea than defending it
September 23, 2008

"Believe me," the letter began. *"We'd rather be just bathing in the sea than constantly defending it."*

The missive arrived from the son of a friend of mine who serves in the Israeli Navy. The young man was honored recently at a ceremony along the seashore, near the port town of Ashdod. The Israeli Navy vociferously patrols the coast up and down the busy beaches, especially in that corridor between the scorched ruins of the terror-infested Gaza City and the gleaming towers of tourist-laden Tel Aviv. My friend's son was cited for valor in one of Israel's countless and obligatory and exhausting interceptions of Palestinian infiltrators who were intent on blowing up a shopping mall, a school, *anything* to prove their nihilistic point.

I had called to express congratulations but missed the thoughtful naval captain, age 22, who would soon complete his service and—as is the ritual of so many young, restless Israeli citizen-soldiers—take off for a year somewhere, anywhere away from the confined, vulnerable, beloved nation-state they are sworn to defend. And it's only after the three-year compulsory service in the army, air force, or navy, and then often after a year to decompress in India or Canada or Thailand, that these lithe, modern Hebrew warriors, replete with iPods, cellular phones, and a hunger to see exotica, even matriculate into one of Israel's many distinguished universities.

We like to glamorize these Israeli men and women (not the politicians, the people) and there is indeed much that is glamorous about them. But our admiration is misplaced, and even our spiritual aura poorly imagined, when we assume that they really want to be cavaliers and spies. They are as tired of the wars, the bombings, the air strikes, the security checks as are the non-indoctrinated young people on the Palestinian side who've not been ruined by the toxic grip of *jihadists*.

My friend's son gave me an important perspective, a harbinger of my Rosh Hashanah devotions, when we will dip apples in honey and pray for the equivalent sweetness for all of God's children. No hero in clay, this tender young man, who saw wrong and tried to right it, who was handed duty and sought to dispense with it.

"Believe me, we'd rather be just bathing in the sea than constantly defending it."

Will this religious new year, this anniversary of Creation, finally be the year of peaceful waters?

I would have gladly served as prison chaplain to the president

September 25, 2008

'NO' was the banner of a large ad and proclamation published in The *New York Times* on Wednesday morning by the United States Holocaust Memorial Museum. The museum, an agency of the federal government (and not, for example, of Jewish auspices), is generally involved in the collecting and preserving of Holocaust artifacts—shoes, eyeglasses, human hair, photos, films, documents, suitcases, lists, concentration camp instruments, poison-gas pellets, Nazi-era Aryan propaganda and anti-Semitic literature, caricatures, and an examination of SS, Gestapo, and Wehrmacht techniques and provisos for the mass destruction of Jews, gypsies, blacks, gays, Catholic priests, sympathizers, and any other "enemies of the Reich."

The museum, dedicated in 1993 by President Bill Clinton, is the official archive and testimonial center of the greatest genocide and wave of "crimes against humanity" in the history of this planet. The Germans, and their inestimable number of cooperatives in several other countries, unspeakably murdered twelve million civilians between 1933 and 1945, particularly six million Jewish men, women, young children, and babies.

But the 'NO' proclaimed by the US Holocaust Museum was not directly associated with the Nazi insanity of World War II. It was a passionate condemnation of the appearance and speech opportunity given at the United Nations to perhaps the most virulent and dangerous and well-armed Holocaust denier and proponent of the destruction of Jewry since Himmler, Eichmann, and Hitler. *Again*, Iranian president Mahmoud Ahmadinejad was cavorting about New York City, making an appearance on *Larry King Live*, and addressing the General Assembly.

The US Holocaust Museum, which is dedicated to preserving the past, was this week frightened for the future. The president of Iran, smug in his anti-Americanism, contemptuous of and foaming over the presence of Israel (the only democracy in the entire Islamic crescent), had ample opportunity to vent, sigh, disingenuously deny his hatred, and generally score a public relations coup just a few subway stops from the profligate Wall Street.

It is perhaps saddest of all—even sadder than the condition of the American spirit—that Ahmadinejad, the son of a blacksmith and, before his national ascent, a mayor, cloaks his toxicity in his Islamic faith. The prophet Mohammed, legendary and essentially inclusive in his sacred teachings, having inspired a new religious culture that categorically respected the ongoing truths of Judaism and Christianity, is not represented well by this postmodern mocker of any civilized nation or spiritual yearning.

Why does our troubled and all-too-good nation tolerate his intrusion, even giving him the bully pulpit of media and assemblies? Why wasn't he just arrested at JFK Airport rather than given credentials and legitimacy?

I'd have gladly served as his prison chaplain, allowing him time to reflect and read something other than his own *Kampf.*

We white folks just don't know what it means to be black

September 26, 2008

As 'Ole Miss' prepares for the presidential debate between two men who represent two different centuries and two different American narratives: *What is it to be black, I wonder?*

How could anyone who isn't black even imagine the yoke of it, the pounding griefs, the relentless degradations, the legacy of slavery and chains and lynchings and unspeakable shackled ocean passages, the mothers and sisters with bowed heads submitting to the avarice of drunken and psychotic white men who measured their sexuality by a sick dominion over African women who had no empowerment, no space on the same continent as the greatest experiment in democracy ever attempted on this planet?

Who could know what James Meredith felt, when he was heinously escorted away from the University of Mississippi and his birthright classrooms by federal marshals in 1963? Who else but another black man could understand, for example, Martin Luther King's obsessive appetite for food, cigarettes, and women, even as he taught the Gospel—unless you are willing to imagine the feeling, every waking moment, of expecting imminent beatings and being jailed repeatedly just because you're asking for what God intended in a civilization? Who could possibly conceive of what Dr. King reportedly knew unequivocally—that he would be murdered exactly as it happened at the Lorraine Motel in Memphis on April 4, 1968?

To live with that, to *know that*, is a burden simply inconceivable to the vast majority of white men in America and something of it, real or perceived, still clings to the collective consciousness of American black men. It doesn't matter if you're a renowned baseball player with genuine philanthropic achievements, a surgeon, a newspaper editor, or a preacher in the century after the Ole Miss segregation: A black man in every one of these categories has personally told me that he has noticed white women pull their purses closer in as he passed by in a mall, or noticed that white families cloistered together or pushed their car's power locks as he walked harmlessly by, thinking about his own kids or how the stock market would affect his portfolio.

I look up at the starry sky, so clear and vivid in black and white. What is it about human nature that some people need to make others smaller? The Germans and what they did to the Jews. The Americans and what we did to the native tribal nations of this new world, even as white Americans wound up killing each other mercilessly between 1861 and 1865 in a Civil War that took more American lives than any other conflict, including World War II. The British and their domination and slaughter of Indians; the incomprehensible caste system of India itself. The Japanese and their butchery of the Chinese, the Turks and their genocide of Armenians, the staggering carnage in the Balkans, Indochina, myriad African wars and famines, the blood of Jerusalem.

This debate is as much about 'who gets it' as it is who wins it.

Legendary actor and philanthropist Paul Newman died the next day (as you shall see); the Jewish High Holy Days were arriving, as well—with their annual rite of repentance, choreography, and inevitable community tensions.

Meanwhile, the upstart Senator Barack Obama of Illinois was full-swing in his presidential campaign against Vietnam veteran and war-horse Senator John McCain. Neither man had been expected to win their respective party nominations at the outset of the painfully long primary and caucus process; in fact, it had been generally assumed that Senator Hillary Clinton would face off against former New York City mayor Rudolph Giuliani.

As 'Spiritual Life Examiner,' I made no distinction between theology, politics, and even the arts—so long as the topic had a spiritual dimension. It was a fall and winter of extraordinary historical ramifications in terms of race, terrorism, democracy, and the changing face of America. Trouble was brewing in India and Gaza, all fueled by dark religious compulsions.

But baseball still had to fulfill its cycle and Halloween, Thanksgiving, and Christmas were still going to draw closer with spook, feast, yuletide, and the sounds and smells of people coming home.

It was '69, Paul Newman was on the screen, and I wanted to kiss Peggy Ellis
September 27, 2008

He was quintessential, lean, and for the teens in my group, Jewishly handsome. You might have thought we boys would resent him for his sinewy coolness, his cold blue eyes, and his trans-ethnic masculinity—we didn't look that good, not usually. But there he was, leading the way in the immortal *Butch Cassidy and the Sundance Kid*, smiling away danger, using his brains and wit to more than match the sun-drenched, gun-toting, casual gentile machismo of Robert Redford's "Sundance."

Newman *was* Butch, the literate, jocular, funny, and focused honcho of the Hole-in-the-Wall Gang—a real outfit that hung on during the receding days of the Old West. He defeated knives with a blindsiding kick to the groin of a man twice his size (and half his intellect) and he negotiated safe-haven deals with sheriffs who begrudged him his insatiable charm.

The only man who could have captured all this guile and brilliance was Paul Newman, the half-Jewish, airy, articulate kid from Shaker Heights, Ohio who never changed: He remained agile, post-Hebrew, and married to the same woman through decades of American churning, religious right-eousness, and declining cinematic standards for the category of "star." Like the actual celestial bodies, you knew that Paul Newman was up there shining, even in the daytime. He didn't have to come out at night for you to remember.

It was 1969, and Paul Newman, transforming the evolving Robert Redford into a legend himself, starred in the original "buddy movie," about Butch and Sundance. I was sixteen, shy, awkward, and desperate for the attention of the raven-haired Peggy Ellis of my high school. Equipped with a driver's license but short on guts, I hadn't yet acquired the nerve to ask the brunette goddess of few words but Natalie Wood looks out to the movies. In those days, you didn't have that much equipment—no cellular, no Internet, no Facebook. It was just your telephone and your gumption.

She said yes to this movie. I sat close to her, taking in her fragrance, even holding her hand. My heart was thumping as Paul Newman effortlessly rode that bicycle past Katharine Ross' window to the sound of B.J.

Thomas singing "Raindrops Keep Falling On My Head." *Nothing* could throw him—or me—off-balance. He won over the girl, the gang, the bank train, and almost got away in Bolivia. Somewhere in between at the old Valley Theater in Cincinnati, I kissed the luscious lips of Peggy Ellis and she squeezed my hand.

It was simple, easy, and divine. And though I've gone on to manhood and mature love, and Paul Newman went on to salad dressings (and NASCAR racing), and his own indignation at the box-office copycats, he was always simple, easy, and divine.

The baseball season and the atonement season play ball

September 28, 2008

Baseball and Bible run together well for this Jewish boy. On this final day of the regular season, it seems natural that the Jewish High Holy Days—the post-season of our faith—are also imminent. The connection, tender and titillating, runs deep for folks like me.

Late Septembers in Cincinnati, humid and historic, are iconographic for those of us who came of age by 1970. With the atonement season came the championship and World Series and the biblical "Big Red Machine" was invariably involved. The Cincinnati Reds won 102 games and the National League pennant in 1970 and were going to face off against a set of Philistines from the American League more commonly known as the Baltimore Orioles.

The Reds, led by the hustling and still pure Pete Rose, and the sturdy, flame-throwing catcher from Oklahoma named Johnny Bench, were not highly favored against the heavy-shouldered Orioles. They had Boog Powell at first, a man of cosmic biceps, the vacuum cleaner third baseman Brooks Robinson at third, the moody but brilliant Frank Robinson in left field (whom the Reds had ignominiously traded in 1966), and a handsome, smooth, mystical pitcher named Jim Palmer.

It was difficult to imagine which was the greater challenge for us boys: Atoning for our sins at Golf Manor Synagogue or the Reds standing up to the O's? An even bigger challenge was *how to listen to the games on the radio during the holiest days of the year.*

We didn't have cellular units, Blackberrys, or anything of the sort. Ah—but I had a prize: The battery-operated and revered Transistor Radio With the Ear Wire. We weren't really comfortable trying to pull a fast one on our dear Rabbi Indich—a scholar and traditionalist with a heart as kind as heaven. But we were not comfortable, either, not knowing what Rose, Bench, Perez, and May were doing on the diamond.

The afternoon service, long and lugubrious, just wouldn't end. So we boys slipped out the back door of the synagogue to the sanctuary of trees along the side of the building. I nervously put the wire in my ear and scoped the small transistor screen for 700 AM (FM was hardly even known yet and generally relegated to eggheads or potheads). The Game! The other boys gathered around me, some of them still donning their flourishing prayer shawls. We looked like a reverse pogrom seeking God in the static.

Then we realized we were not alone. The shadow of the rather tall, bearded, red-haired Rabbi Indich, his left leg crooked from diabetes, his blue eyes ablaze with fervor, made me realize that I was headed for a scriptural strikeout. The other boys couldn't even run—they were frozen with fear. The wire popped out of my ear.

"Kamin, is that you listening to the game?"

I absolutely knew that my religious life was over.

"Yes, Rabbi."

"Well, then, what's the score?" The rabbi smiled and I knew that God is good. The Reds, incidentally, were not.

Jesus returns home at Rosh Hashanah
September 29, 2008

At the Jewish New Year, Jesus has returned to his roots. In his own mortal lifetime, the brilliant and charismatic teacher spoke Hebrew, offered devotions from Jewish traditions, shared and adapted Talmudic maxims, and particularly reiterated the spiritual aphorisms of the eminent teaching master Hillel—the preeminent scholar and sage of rabbinic Judaism. Hillel lived 100 years before Jesus.

In his all-too-brief 30 years as a human being in ancient Judea, Jesus emulated the populist overtones of the Hebrew prophets, eschewing hypocrisy and rote rituals in favor of sincere prayers and social justice. The actual title of "rabbi" did not exist during the lifespan of this courageous young man who took on both the Romans and the calcified Jewish establishment; this moniker was conferred later on Christ, as was the notion of his resurrection and paternal relationship to God.

Jesus was a consummate Jew, as so many Christians know, honor, and even celebrate. It was the extraordinary Saul (later renamed Paul) who—*one hundred years after the crucifixion of this noble teacher*—had an absolute epiphany on the road to Damascus. Paul's sincerity and conviction are beyond doubt, and historically inviolate, particularly when news of Jesus' messianic ministry spread into the Roman Empire.

But Jesus was a Jew named Joshua and he'd feel very comfortable with his Jewish community at this time in any temple or synagogue. We are asking God for a renewal of the earth and its environment, we are pleading for world peace, and we are praying for the inspiration and integrity to actually forgive others. We are entreating God for those in need, the shut-ins, the widowed, the infirm, the countless human souls who trudge through so many forms of anonymous suffering. We are being reminded that we are all God's children.

What would Jesus do if he were visiting during Rosh Hashanah, the mystical birth of the world, and the anniversary of creation? Hopefully, joining us and our congregation for the very liturgies he learned as a child and then interpreted as a visionary young man.

October, 2008

Why can't folks feel comfortable—no, feel exalted—by the notion that God didn't write the Bible? Men and women inspired by God wrote these stirring and sacred stories that need moral follow-through much more than factual verification.

The best Bible moments that you don't know about
October 1, 2008

The Sunday School teachers too often emphasized the big miracles, the partings of seas, the cataclysmic plagues, the terrible thunder and lightning. Better we should glean the true beauty of Scripture from those many smaller moments, when somebody touched somebody's face, when a lover wept, when a young man felt spirituality, or when a young woman, caught in the crossfire of war, feared for her life.

I'm thinking today of that anonymous woman, from ancient Israel to today's Iraq. Known—and lobbied for—in the Torah as "the female captive," she is perhaps comely, perhaps not. The real issue for her is the incongruous and unleashed brutality of men smashing through her town, her fields, her hut, her world, with their spears raised, their rage foaming, their standards obliterated by the chaos of battle, power, and lust.

To its unending credit, the Hebrew Scripture addresses this matter to the *Hebrew* warriors who would charge Canaan, and, according to the biblical directives, conquer and subdue the Promised Land. "When you go to war," Moses tells them, speaking for God, there were certain rules and constraints—these coded three thousand years before Abu Ghraib.

The Hebrew soldiers were ordered to *go around* orchards and olive groves—even while in pursuit of the enemy. The earth and its harvests were still more important than strategic battle objectives. This understanding of what war does to men with weapons, how it not only takes lives but obliterates the meaning of life, is more important to me than so many divine floods, earthquakes, and thunderbolts.

And then Moses tells them how to behave if they capture a woman and desire her for a wife. The soldiers are told that they may *not* wantonly seize her. They are instructed to let her retire to her home, wash her face, brush her hair, trim her fingernails, and, most poignantly, be given time to "cry for her father's house." After that, when she emerges, perhaps the soldier will reconsider this woman not as an object but as a human being who trembles with dread, misses her home, and has dignity. But not only that: If the victorious combatant comes to tire of his captive, he can't just throw her out. He must return her to her parents' home and let her go gracefully.

Someday, the nations, including our own beloved America, will realize that our real strength is measured exactly by how we treat the weakest.

Part 2: The Jews don't reject Jesus personally, just the whole idea
October 2, 2008

Some years ago, a brilliant and ingratiating Christian woman—devout, artistic, formerly a soap opera television star, married happily to a leading Jewish philanthropist and major sports team owner in the Midwest—asked me about Jesus. "So you don't believe in his divinity?" It was not a leading question; she had respect and was secure enough in her sustaining belief not to be threatened or pugnacious in any response. no matter what the response.

No, not in his divinity, I answered. But I went on to explain that his place in theological history is inviolate and that Christianity has been, and remains, the defining faith of western civilization, and that it has helped a lot of people. Moreover, the notion of a celestial figure who expressed the rhapsody, even the angst of God, among human beings, is appealing and sublime. The Hebrew Scripture includes several other such figures, including Moses and Samuel and Deborah—but they all were mortal. They lived and died and, in between, were *inspired* and invigorated by their perception of God to help repair the world. They were not *related* to God, nor did they die to exonerate other people's weaknesses. They were people who saw things that others did not, said things that others could not even imagine, and they died for principles.

My friend's eyes twinkled and I actually envied her unyielding faith in her messianic beacon that sheltered her, it seemed, in the wings of his ministry. She was kind, and then modified her inquiry: "Can you believe then, in the *tenderness* of Jesus?" "I love that idea," was my genuine response, and have even employed it to explain the concept of Jesus for Christians to skeptical or even downright myopic Jews—and others. Tenderness is good; human divinity is blurry.

My Christian friends understand that Judaism is not based on the rejection of Jesus. In the first place, Judaism existed for millennia before Jesus; he himself was a Jew who elucidated apocalyptic visions and gave people hope in the time of bestial Roman subjugation. Jews reject the idea that *any person* can become God, or part of God. There were others who came along through the centuries, such as the medieval Sabbatai Zvi, who claimed to be the messiah, and were summarily dismissed. None of them, however, offered the tenderness of the man Jesus.

Christians who disparage Jews as Christ-rejecters, or Christ-killers, only offer a pejorative—and sometimes homicidal—skewing of the Talmudic-based canons of Jesus. Nor are Jews "incomplete Christians." We parented Christianity and are proud of our literature, our theology, our array of biblical characters who are beloved by both communities. But our heroes were flawed, they had good days and bad days, they loved some and hurt others, they doubted and then embraced God. They got angry, petty, and they sometimes prayed very hard; none of them had a blood connection to God, nor were they perfect.

It's the very earth-solid notion that no one can be perfect, no one can do things that only the heavenly God does, that keeps Jews, religious or not, grounded in two ways: We can live with our own blemishes and we can forgive yours.

Judaism is sociology; Christianity is faith
October 8, 2008

In other denominations, confession is a personal event, often realized between the confessor and a priestly intermediary. The cleric is charged with admonition but also the release, by virtue of so many devotions, mantras and other rituals.

Not so with the Jews: As the community gathers to complete the rites of the New Year, large groups are forming, mostly in congregational settings. Rosh Hashanah was celebrated as the birthday of the world, Creation's anniversary, when God separated elements, such as water and firmament, and made the Earth.

We dipped apples in honey, tasting the fruits and sweetness of this world, smacking our lips with hope and renewal. We were all doing the same thing—from Tarzana to Tel Aviv. The themes of repentance and contrition were introduced, but not fully engaged until the more severe and ascetic and fast day of Yom Kippur. We're committed to the notion that God is preparing a judgment about us that is sealed in the legendary Book of Life.

Nearly every prayer, entreaty and appeal in the thick prayer book of these "Days of Awe" is in the plural form. "Our Father, Our King, we have sinned against you... " The climactic, sorrowful and poignant *Kol Nidrei* of Yom Kippur Eve is a national cry: "Let all the vows we made from last year to this year that we did not fulfill be null and void!" Surely, every individual is charged to make peace with others (the primary goal of the season, in fact), but the experience is *plural, communal and collective.*

Jews don't go to their rabbi to confess sins in a private, cloaked setting—though this is a powerful process that has helped a lot of people. The rabbi has no authority or leverage with the angels other than the ability to inspire good works. The very word "rabbi" means "teacher." There is no greater title in Jewish history; we have always eschewed kings and lieges in favor of prophets and sages.

So in this season of turning leaves and changing breezes, of solstice and star shine, when even birds and trees revolve along with human beings, when the air is a bit sharper with autumnal reflection, we come together for warmth and consolation.

Unlike our Christian neighbors, we are redeemed as a group. For the good Christian, it's a question of *"I can be saved."* For the Jew, burnished by history, longing for the ancestral peoplehood that heard the ram's horn as a tribe and made pilgrimage to Jerusalem, it's a matter of *"We can be saved."* This is not judgmental, it is simply observational.

We left Egypt together, we received the Law at Sinai together, we entered the Promised Land together, we were finally exiled by the Romans together. We yearned together for a return to Zion, we suffered brutish exiles and wanton Inquisitions together, we perished in the Holocaust together, we restored the state of Israel together.

When a Jew visits Buenos Aires or London or Athens, the first thing he or she does is go look for the local synagogue or the premier Jewish delicatessen. A Christian may tour churches, and he may scout out good food, but he is not looking for that indelible, blood-drenched link between himself and the local manifestation of the remnant. When I'm in Rome, I cherish my visits in the Vatican and honor the reverence of the place. I weep in the Sistine Chapel. But I've already been to the Jewish Ghetto and tasted the time-honored Jewish artichoke sautéed in oil that connects me to my ghosts.

Judaism is sociology; Christianity is liturgy. Christianity is a faith; Judaism is a people with a faith. The Jewish New Year is not just a devotion; it's a national meeting.

Tonight and tomorrow, we also thank God, in specific prayers, for the privilege of our freedom to pray in this blessed America.

On the holiest day, this Jew told her to 'Go back to China!'
October 10, 2008

He survived the Nazis as a teenager in France, and he claims to be fiercely proud of his heritage. But on Yom Kippur, in the midst of a litany of forgiveness and atonement, Henry forgot everything that his life might have taught him. During a break in our afternoon liturgy, after hours of contrite and peace-seeking prayers, after all the music and poetry of mercy, this fierce old man defiled everything that filled our temple and defined our mission.

Walking past Henrietta, our brilliant and much-beloved choir director, a classical pianist and conductor who came to this great country long ago from China, Henry blasted: "You should go back to China!" Never mind that Henry had been singing devotions for literally days that filled the hall poignantly under the artistic direction of this lovely and creative woman who is the heart and soul of our choral group. Never mind that this Asian woman of deep Christian piety knows more Hebrew than Henry and that she, in one of her famous smiling embraces of anyone in the congregation, displays more tenderness than her attacker could even conjure up in his wounded mind.

Never mind that the Jewish tradition is anchored by the following ancient rabbinic command: "What is hateful to you, do not do to any other person."

Henrietta, dignified, often so funny, with impeccable standards, came to me and broke into tears. She leaned into my white robe and sobbed: "I'm not even wearing my Cross today." My anguish and pain doubled as I recalled, indeed, that this was not the first time our troubled and misguided congregant had so egregiously assailed this gentle woman.

Months ago, he approached her during a choir rehearsal and incomprehensibly vilified her for wearing her necklace, blurting out unforgivable things about the symbol she wore across her neck. At that time, I personally warned Henry that such blatant bigotry will not be tolerated under any circumstances and that any member of our staff—and indeed anyone at all—who wears the Cross in our congregation is as much a part of God's family as anyone else.

I admonished him sternly that, while I respect his personal history, the Cross has historically been a sign of peace and that his words and actions only mimicked those who had desecrated the symbol in the name of violence. "Words, too, can kill," I cautioned the grim man, quoting again from the Jewish tradition.

This gray morning after Yom Kippur, I am so troubled and saddened. Yes, Henry suffered unspeakable things under the Vichy-sponsored detention camp he survived in World War II. But he is free to read from the Torah (as he has) in our blessed America, and his very experiences should inform him viscerally how destructive such wanton prejudice is.

I have to ponder now and decide what to recommend to our temple leadership about Henry's future in our congregation. What shall I do? How to turn back what one cycle of cruelty has done to nurture a second wave of malice?

One thing for sure: If music has died in one person's heart, it will still be made by another, so long as I represent the Jewish people.

The moon, the mosque, God, and the Girl Scouts
October 12, 2008

When I beheld the full moon and knew that the Jewish fall festival of Sukkot was about to glow, I gave new thought to the fact that my Muslim neighbors in the community were equally spellbound by the moon—also for reasons of the spirit. Several days ago, after sharing lentil soup and fresh dates with pious men and a proud troop of Girl Scouts at the Islamic Center of our city, the moon took on another face for me—and my step-children were able to put a face on their perceptions of Islam.

Keenly aware of the lunar calendar (as are we Jews), Imam Amir joined this past month's Ramadan rituals to his concerns about interfaith relations and outreach. Without much fanfare and with his trademark quiet grace, the Imam extended an invitation to a number of non-Muslim faith leaders to come to the Islamic Center recently and share in the *iftar*—the evening breakfast that occurs daily at sundown during this ninth and especially sacred month of the twelve-month Islamic calendar.

My wife, the two teenage children, and I, curious, eager, hungry, arrived at the Islamic Center at the announced time of 6:15 PM, a yellow sun regally crowning the gathering dusk against the mosque dome and crescent. An exotic holiness filled the air; the feathery clouds, tinged with color, the forgiving evening breeze, and the gathering worshippers, most of them men, all greeted us with warmth and gratitude. It didn't seem as though the devotees and volunteers of the mosque generally expect people like us to walk in and share their traditions, sensibilities, and pita bread.

We were the only Jewish folks—and I was certainly the only native Israeli—amongst the forty or so guests, Christian, Sikh, Hindu, that were personally welcomed by Imam Amir in a pleasantly cool and colorfully decorated classroom that included a generously laden buffet table of salads, chicken, lamb, eggplant, baba ghanoush, hummus, and tahina sauces. "Isn't this Israeli food?" asked my stepson, his red hair and big eyes thick with excitement and the kind of innocent curiosity that belies everything we've more or less resigned ourselves to in the category of world affairs and international failure. "Yes, it's the same things I ate in Israel," I replied, "because so much Israeli food is actually Arab food." A few moments later, Imam Amir, so relaxed and proud of his communal accomplishment, teased me: He is from Egypt and he wondered if "perhaps you and I once swam in the same sea at some time."

We all devoured thick bowls of lentil soup in a transitional moment before prayer and the subsequent main meal. I thought about the biblical Isaac's favoring of this same soup and the fact that his father was the same Abraham cherished as the ancestral father of both Jews and Muslims. My step-daughter, blonde, suburban, and conscientious, made notes for her "Islam" school project while taking in the colorful garbs and interesting faces of so many faiths and cultures who were being nourished that night by a smiling moon and a healing cycle.

She followed her mother and the other women to a berth above the center's mosque while my stepson and I joined the other males on the floor of the worship hall. We had been taken there by the wailing call to prayer. The two hundred Muslim men successively bowed and prostrated themselves; we guests watched from a small distance and took in the mantra. My boy remarked on the thickness of the carpet and we whispered to each other about the appealing austerity of a divine house without furniture where souls seemed to find comfortable places to rest.

Upstairs again, we feasted—a mosaic of happy guests and mindful hosts who truly yearned for our approval and the consoling effect of their deeply sincere hospitality. It was not necessary to solicit our delight—we were touched and informed and softened by the good food and cheerful spirits. The more Imam Amir talked to me about the themes of forgiveness and renewal inherent within Ramadan, the more I revisited my own people's New Year festival just unfolding. The moon, the fast, the devotions of mercy and atonement aligned with my own faith and I could only wonder why, really *why*, the common children of Abraham did not realize that we more than breathe the same air and want the same for our children.

Not the answer, but certainly a ray of hope, came from the zealous troop of in-house mosque Girl Scouts, replete with uniforms, troop badges, and "Share Ramadan With A Friend" patches, who distributed boxes of dates to all the visitors. The young ladies, mingling with us among the Arabic prayers posted on the walls, the scientific posters about hydrogen, photosynthesis, and the solar system, spoke to us more than anything: Our generation, even Amir and myself, will likely not see such a table set in Jerusalem, Algiers, Baghdad, or Beirut. But thanks to the courage of men like Amir, and the purity of a patch of Muslim girl scouts who pass out fresh dates, some of us will never see the moon again in quite the same way.

Angels: Turn off your cell phones while in the sky, please

October 13, 2008

Some of the hard-pressed commercial airlines are again working with federal regulators on a plan to permit passengers to talk on cellular phones at any time during a flight. Technicians would install a small cell tower, pizza-box shaped, inside the jet that would disseminate the signals. *Oy vey*—the ministering angels up in the heavens must be having a group cyber-fit: How will they conduct business with all those banal conversations now shirt-circuiting the clouds and firmament?

Even saints and seraphs are entitled to freedom from second-hand-cell.

And what good will this do us blabby mortals, already addicted and transfixed by wireless units on earth? You won't be able to order a delivery pizza while flying from Orlando to Denver, but you will be able to make the passenger seated next to you crazy by calling your mother in Omaha while you're bored above Michigan to tell her that the airline chicken you just had was cold and tasteless. This is pertinent information that may drive some of us to buy stock in companies that make anti-noise head-phones. (Sorry, I didn't mean to mention stocks.)

I suppose we all sensed this coming during the cellular tension of every airplane landing. The flight attendants used to announce that the use of cellular phones was prohibited until the aircraft had reached the gate and the cabin door was open. Nobody really paid attention, so the flight attendants mostly gave in. Now most even specify within seconds of touchdown that "you can use your cell phone now."

Beep! Bell! Bolero! Now we've got Schubert's Unnecessary Symphony of Self-Importance. Nobody can get up, nobody can light a cigarette, nobody can even think of touching the dangerous overhead compartment because contents may have shifted and people could be mauled by malcontent briefcases and grumpy knapsacks. But you can freely turn on a transmitting beam that may seriously disrupt cockpit communications and tell somebody what he or she already read on a home PC or a BlackBerry: You've landed.

This information is as newsworthy as it is redundant. What does your spouse think, that you're in Atlanta when you are expected in Cincinnati at 11:37?

If the airlines are going to surrender to consumer indulgence and give away any semblance of privacy or peacefulness on board their overstuffed 737s and Airbuses, then perhaps they will agree to a compromise: Let only the people who are in the middle seats, not aisle or window, be allowed to use their phones. The only condition is that the middle passenger, while being granted unlimited lavatory access along with unlimited minutes, has to make and take calls for people in the aisle or window positions. Every middle seat on every plane in this country will remain unoccupied under these conditions and the rest of us will do what we want to do anyway while in flight: sleep and forget all that awaits us in Houston.

This call should not go through. The angels know what we are saying anyway—why shout it in their ears?

A prior version of this piece appeared in the
Los Angeles Times.

Jesus, if today is the Second Coming, please come to my sukkah
October 14, 2008

In one of the most thrilling permutations of Christianity and Judaism, the Second Coming of Jesus, is generally understood as being scheduled for the Jewish fall harvest festival, Sukkot. Since Sukkot—the sweet holiday of the little huts—begins today, I'd like to personally invite Jesus to come back via my humble *sukkah* and share in some of our family fruits, breads, and wine. Isn't such a place the tenderest of entries, grander than any grand sanctuary, freer than any canonized institution?

As is written in the Book of John, "If anyone is thirsty, let him come to me and drink." In the Hebrew Scripture, Zechariah describes Sukkot as a kind of final "harvest of souls." Meanwhile, this Jew is hardly threatened and actually would be elated if a messianic event could indeed take place and unconditionally wed all Jews and Christians in a reconciliation that transcends both religions and sends us all back to God.

And what better place than within a simple yard tabernacle? (OK, if mine isn't suitable, any tabernacle will do, as long as we all grasp hands and celebrate the joy of redemption). The prophet Micah, beloved by all, promised that we'd all know the great peace when God will again "tabernacle" with His people.

The *sukkah*, with frail walls that welcome fresh air, and that shut no one out with locks, bolts, and security systems, is the only dwelling place suitable for any Redeemer. Here we gather together, transparent and happy, visible to our neighbors, and we bless the grains and the produce of the earth and the warmth of sunshine. If it rains upon us, we are only grateful that the soils are replenished and the seeds of future blossoms are nourished.

In the little hut, there is no coaxial connection, no television, no Internet, no wires of any kind that import the noise and indoctrinations of the outside world into the sanctity of our quiet conversations and our gentle songs. At night, the thatched roof lets in not only the star shine and invigorating fall air, but also the visiting souls of our common ancestors, Abraham and Sarah, Isaac and Rebekah, Jacob, Leah, and Rachel.

For eight days that both the Old and New Testaments anoint as worthy of a messiah, there are, thankfully, no political polls, no Dow Jones, no Nielsen ratings, or theological manipulation. Just apples, lentils, repasts, spices, hanging artwork by kids, study, and psalms of praise. No wonder Jesus regards this old Jewish holiday as his natural landing place.

I love it when Jews and Christians are tripping all over one another with the same texts and dreams. Enjoy your little hut, or, if you don't have one, go and create it with someone.

From the Angel of Death to the Jewish dybbuk, Hallowe'en is for everybody!

October 15, 2008

Years ago, four Orthodox Jewish boys, defying the traditional Jewish proscription on Hallowe'en, bravely snuck out anyway. At dusk they emerged, practically floating with delight, grasping little brown lunch bags for their candies, out for "Trick or Treat" in the old neighborhood. It was if they had been set free to experience something dark and mysterious and forbidden—that also resulted in a heap of Snickers, M&Ms, Mars Bars, Reese's Cups, Twizzlers, and Pink Dubble Bubble Gum like these fundamentalists had never imagined. The small change they got they immediately turned back over to their synagogue!

We were all about twelve, and I knew those curly-locked fellows, though I ran with the more secular-culture crowd of Jews and Catholics in the neighborhood. Frankly, I didn't even know back then what the fuss was about not participating in a holiday that some in my community called "pagan," and others excoriated because it derived from a "Hallows' Eve." Fine—for me it was about a brisk night of safe carousing, spooky swirling leaves, hot cider, lighted grinning pumpkins and it was not negotiable.

The record shows that my identity was not affected and I have great memories and shared a heady experience in a charming, departed neighborhood with fellows named Schuster, Smith, and O'Reilly. We dressed up as goblins, skeletons, and ball players and, after divvying up and devouring our loot of chocolate bars, had the appropriate stomachaches on the first morning of November.

Why the reluctance, the disapproving hang-up among some Jews (and other groups) about this gilded fall milestone? Meanwhile, the Jewish biblical and post-biblical traditions are the ones *loaded* with ghouls, ghosts, and evil spirits.

What kind of Exodus from Egypt could be recorded absent the malevolent and gurgling Angel of Death that came for the Egyptian first-born? Witches? What of the legendary Lilith, Adam's supposed first flame, who, with long hair and flaming eyes, beguiled and seduced men in their sleep?

And there is the unforgettable and terrifying superhero, the Golem, a Frankenstein-like ogre that evolved from clay and was completely supernatural. Nor would Jewish literary and social history be complete without the perennial *dybbuk*—described by one contemporary writer as "an evil spirit that seeks vulnerable souls to displace so that it can occupy a person's body." Only exorcism can rid one of the *dybbuk*. Watch the beloved *Fiddler on the Roof* and you will be chilled by the extended paranormal scene of aroused corpses dancing and prophesying during Tevye's cemetery dream—*oy vey*.

These aren't mainstream images but neither are the once-a-year specters and terrors and shrieks of the wickedly fun Hallowe'en season. What's the moral here? My four Orthodox-garbed friends got the most loot in their bags that night, outdoing all of us, because without even changing, they were already in the most elaborate costumes! Hallowe'en is culture with hot cider and a good fright. Trick or treat—amen.

No debate: Jesse Jackson should examine his soul

October 16, 2008

Rev. Jesse Jackson has something that, at once, has always been both his greatest strength and greatest weakness—his mouth. Yesterday, continuing to demonstrate his inexorable coveting of Sen. Barack Obama, he again shot off remarks that were disruptive, wounding, and basically untrue. So gifted an orator, so inspiring a leader through much of his storied career, he has nonetheless brought gloom to the collective spirit of people who are just trying to bring other people together.

A mega-ego often dispels a good spirit. Yesterday, Jackson, who has helped a lot of people, claimed that a possible Obama presidency would realign US foreign policy—a good thing, if we regain the respect and admiration of the family of nations. But the reverend also mangled his promising declaration by then zeroing in on "the Zionists" who will likely have less clout under a more neutral Obama administration (according to the reverend). Whatever our policy is *vis a vis* our unyielding ally and intelligence partner Israel, this was yet another cheap shot at the Jews—a pattern maintained by the Gospel preacher over some time now.

When Rev. Jackson was overheard on a live microphone disparaging Obama several months ago, wishing he could cut off the candidate's genitals, people of all backgrounds were horrified. His own son, Congressman Jesse Jackson, Jr., publicly decried and excoriated his Dad for the outrage. Whither thy spirit, Reverend?

Rev. Martin Luther King, Jr. had mixed feelings about his then young and muscular associate. There was always a strain between them because Dr. King recognized Jackson's mountainous ambition as well as his considerable skills. Jackson notoriously claimed for years that he was among those who actually cradled the dying King on the balcony of Lorraine Motel in Memphis after the fatal shot at 6:00 PM on April 4, 1968. Rev. Samuel "Billy" Kyles would beg to differ—he wrapped an orange blanket around his lifeless friend, there outside Room 306.

In fact, Jesse Jackson was one floor below, at street level, and King had just called out to him before the assassination. Jackson made quick flight to the death scene, dipped his shirt in King's blood (for both spiritual and theatrical reasons) and then was vividly available to the media in the hours after the unspeakable tragedy.

And yet: Jackson, by his sheer dynamism and daunting physical presence (I was one of his co-officiants at the funeral, in 1996, of Cleveland Mayor Carl B. Stokes), can make a claim as Dr. King's public successor in African-American leadership. That is exactly why he should consider his theology before releasing his vanity. Ironically, he became the first serious African-American contender for the Democratic presidential nomination in the 1980s—paving the way for this historic election when both a black man and a woman are on the national ballot.

Jesse, you did so well—can't you find the serenity you need to finally set yourself free?

That fall, indeed, Jesse Jackson receded, though he shed sincere years at the Democratic National Convention when a certain, thin, grandiloquent senator from Illinois was nominated for president. The dream—and memory—of Martin Luther King, Jr. seem to live again in the person of the young man who finished the 1963 cry of "I have a dream!" with the 2008 avowal of "Yes, we can!"

The Elvis stamp? Return to sender

October 17, 2008

One of those remarkable people called a 'philatelist' visited me the other day with a voluminous collection of stamps. This fellow, who even carries around a special moist sponge for his stamps ("It's so crass to lick a stamp," he snarls), is actually a member of the American Philatelic Society. He is very disappointed in the current lack of artistic merit in U.S. stamps, and is opposed to the self-sticking variety. He takes great pride in his anthology of cancelled samples and really possesses a pronounced sense of history and citizenship.

But when he pulled out a commemorative first class stamp with the visage of **Elvis Presley,** we got into a bit of a tussle. I opposed the Elvis stamp, released by the Postal Service in 1993, although I adored Elvis and particularly admired his unabashed admiration for black-style vocalization. But Elvis Presley should not have a stamp in his memory. You can love Elvis, you can know every lyric of his haunting ballads, but you can still sense that there is something wrong with engraving this tragic man on our letters and cards.

Elvis Presley died ignominiously and self-abusively. He killed himself with drugs, alcohol, and indulgence. The end of his life came to be a cacophony of blind extravagance and gross irresponsibility. He was not martyred; he was stoned. Elvis Presley, brilliant, stunning, original, nevertheless became as sick in spirit was he was sublime in song. His music was good; his lifestyle was bad. Can't we acknowledge the difference? At the time of the release of the Presley stamp, some officials of the Postal Service did acknowledge the concerns of educators and psychologists who mentioned the poor role model Elvis had become—as well as the culture of Elvis "sightings" and reincarnations that blur the difference between life and death for kids. This continues to be a problem against the background of the national epidemic of teenage suicide. Kids are playing dangerous games with their health because they don't always get it that death is final.

In the end, the Postal Service, always poorly run, and fiscally dysfunctional, decided to run the stamp and enjoy its biggest sales of any stamp in history. Never mind the ramifications of putting the stamp of approval on an idol who surely would have never wanted any youngster to pursue the kind of self-destruction that he did. I don't want a dead Elvis on a stamp; better a live Elvis on a stage. Remember when the government canted the refrain, "Just say no!"?

An earlier version of this article appeared in
The New York Times.

God did not write the Bible, thank God
October 19, 2008

When we were children, and somebody opened a Bible for us, we didn't have to worry much about where the words fit in history. So, Adam and Eve came into our lives through the lovely garden. Noah collected the animals, two by two, and it rained long enough for the ark to float for forty days. Moses climbed up Mt. Sinai and received two tablets of the Law. God parted the Red Sea so the Israelites could flee to freedom; the Egyptians drowned in their own chariots.

On that last one, even the Jewish fundamentalists admonish us to feel the woe of the Egyptians—"for they were also God's children." So much for God being the author, if the pious must edit. Not to mention the two consecutive conflicting accounts of Creation, the significant pattern of chronological mistakes, the clear differences in writing style that permeate the text. Deuteronomy reads a lot like Isaiah (who lived much later); the Gospels have a variety of differences in terms of narrative and detail.

Thank God! I don't want the most sublime literature to have been imported to earth from heaven. Why can't folks feel comfortable—no, feel exalted—by the notion that God didn't write the Bible? Men and women *inspired by God* wrote these stirring and sacred stories that need moral follow-through much more than factual verification.

Why would God create a world in which there is no poetry, no imagination, no healthy rebellion and spirit in the souls of people? Don't get stuck on the divine authorship; let your reaction and good works to these holy dramas be divine. Remember how the human soul works: The power of story transcends the literal value of what is being told or taught.

People need instructive legends to help religion fly (without anybody getting hurt)—this has been true from Egypt to Greece to Israel to Rome to America. If we accept, as grownups, that George Washington probably did not cut down a cherry tree, but still accept the national fatherhood of our first president, why would we accord less to Moses the lawgiver or to David the King or to Deborah the prophet-commander?

Whether or not Moses actually made footprints on Sinai takes nothing away from what Sinai teaches us. Whether or not David composed all of the

Psalms takes nothing away from their rhapsody, their painful beauty, their healing consolation. God is my help, not my author. I give human beings too much credit for creativity, ideas, anger, reconciliation, to make us all into robots when it comes to the most venerated literature of all time!

Did the Bible really happen?

Better to make sure it is simply *happening*.

"I'm afraid there are guns between me and the White House"

October 21, 2008

Gov. Sarah Palin spoke effectively and responsibly Sunday when she called upon her supporters at rallies to tone down the threatening rhetoric. It was a clear acknowledgment of the occasional shouts of *"We don't want him"* and even *"Kill him!"* that have been directed at Sen. Barack Obama during McCain and Palin speeches.

Without making a fuss about it, I have had a life-long connection with the civil rights movement, its history, and have had the privilege of talking with some its past leaders in both the white and black communities. There are some who are not reticent: They fear for the safety of Barack Obama. I have dear friends who support John McCain for president (and their blessed right to do so is actually more important than either of the candidates) and they share the same genuine concern.

There are some folks in the African-American community who are actually conflicted about the ascendancy of Sen. Obama. They are proud, ecstatic, and they will vote for him. But a part of them don't want him to get too many votes because these veterans of the 1950s and 1960s live with nightmares about dreadful possibilities.

Ironically, the chilling comparison they make is not so much with the murder of Dr. King, on April 4, 1968. It's certainly as much with the shooting down of Sen. Robert F. Kennedy, the brother of martyred President John F. Kennedy, who ran for president and was assassinated on June 5 that same year.

Bobby Kennedy was 42 and was considered an inspirational, transitional figure in that daunting year of 1968—during a detested war, the retirement of an unpopular president, and a racially embroiled season. After losing King, and seeing cities on fire, black folks saw Robert F. Kennedy as their last hope.

Bobby Kennedy personally and bravely informed a large, predominantly black crowd in Indianapolis that Dr. King had just been murdered in Memphis: *"I know something of what you feel…I also had a relative and he was killed by a white man."* He urged them to honor King's memory by not turning to violence. Remarkably, Indianapolis was the only major city not to erupt in rioting that terrible night.

A few days later, Hosea Williams, a close King aide, said to Kennedy: "You have a chance to be a prophet. But prophets get shot."

We don't know if Bobby Kennedy would have been a true prophet and we don't know yet if Barack Obama will be president. We do know that Kennedy sensed something in his troubled country; he would come to say: "I'm afraid there are guns between me and the White House."

For the sake of the soul of our nation, let current history unfold without shouting, without bloodlust, and please God, without Robert Kennedy's prophecy coming true.

Part 2: The Elvis Syndrome, turning death into kitsch
October 23, 2008

When celebrities "live on" past their deaths or suicides, then how they died and the very fact of their mortality can be lost upon our impressionable young people. I want kids to be *scared* of the way Elvis Presley or Kurt Cobain died; instead, the cyber-profit culture encourages a kind of national séance with Elvis.

"Sightings" are reported from hamburger joints, radio stations, and mini-malls. If Elvis lives, or if John Lennon's image can be reincarnated by electronic magic on a Beatles compact disc, then maybe these two victims — one of self-abuse, the other of murder—aren't really dead.

The message this sends to vulnerable teenagers is that death is not necessarily final and that fatal practices do not necessarily extract a grim penalty. In the world of posthumous fame," a major newspaper stated, "a celebrity's death need not impinge on his or her marketability." I am worried about this because most teenagers have enough of a hard time with their awareness of mortality. Making it seem as though death is not final may bring in profits for entertainment lawyers, estate experts, and copyright specialists. It's not so good for kids who understand very little about royalties but a lot about night terror, and who are coping with helpless, even suicidal, feelings.

After Kurt Cobain killed himself in 1994, a management consultant was quoted as saying: "I definitely think he's going to have legs." As a media move, it was great. We shouldn't "give legs" to the rising notion of susceptible young people that death is not a terminal condition. Is life a television soap opera where people who have been murdered or die (still looking rosy) from terrible illnesses return with refurnished contracts and renewed plotlines?

Or isn't life—real life—the place where, according to the Children's Defense Fund, 1 in 6 young people between the ages of 10 and 17 has seen or knows someone who has been shot? It may be cool to purchase freeze-dried "Elvis sweat," but the fact is that in the United States, children under 18 (according to the FBI) are 244% more likely to be killed by guns now than they were in 1986. Now, *this is not Elvis Presley's fault*; it's the fault of the commercialism and retail idolatry that may have contributed to the sweet singer's own self-destruction. Record moguls, movie producers, Internet manipulators, and others (including some parents) have forgotten what their own trembling was like, at the age of 12 or 13, when they suddenly realized that life will end someday and that the end of the discussion is nothing but the grave.

There is a teenage suicide epidemic in this country. We all have to act as though death is not only not glamorous—it is very dark.

My Uncle Moshe knew more about death than all the sages

October 24, 2008

One of the reasons we sometimes believe we've heard from the dead is our obvious and understandable concern for their safety and where-abouts. After my father died suddenly in 1976, I kept wondering where he actually was. I was 23 years old at the time and profoundly affected. It was even harder for my younger brother and sister, and, of course, our still-young mother. None of us were prepared for this abrupt and brazen intrusion of the mortal facts of life.

But I kept wondering, where is my father now? An answer came from an unlikely source: My uncle, my mother's brother, who arrived from Israel to help us in our sorrow. My Uncle Moshe had never flown in an airplane prior to this quickly organized mercy mission.

To this day, Moshe, now in his 80's, is not a particularly reverential man. I don't think that he prays very much, and he has suffered much himself, including the loss of his middle boy to heart problems some years after my father. Meanwhile, Moshe has fought in enough of the Middle East wars to make him generally skeptical about human nature.

But my Uncle Moshe, a kind of post-Zionist Tevye the Milkman, does believe in the idea of heaven, and he certainly believed in my father—who was his dear friend. I asked my uncle, as we walked under the stars one night: "Moshe, where is my father now?" Moshe thought about it for a moment, wrinkling his brow, blowing out smoke from his omnipresent un-filtered cigarette. Finally he spoke:

"He's in a good place."

"How do you know that?" I retorted.

"Tell me something." My uncle focused on me. "Your father was very particular and he didn't have patience for trivialities. If it wasn't a good place, don't you think he'd come back?"

This bit of raw theology has helped me over the years. I understand that Uncle Moshe's response amounted to a bit of folk formulation on life and death, but it was very tender and intuitive. The notion that my father would come back if he was unhappy has continued to give me a measure of comfort and a chuckle over the course of time.

What could be better than that, in view of the facts of life?

My first funeral was, well, an open-and-shut case

October 26, 2008

As I walked into the ornate funeral home in Wabash, Indiana, I found, much to my surprise, that the first person I would meet was none other than Max Reingold. This wasn't so good: Max Reingold was the deceased. It was 1977, I was a student rabbi performing my first-ever funeral; Max Reingold had died in Los Angeles and was back home. This all wasn't working out so well for me.

Max lay in state, his nearly century-old body already flaky and gray from the week's travel and relocation. This was a shock to me, but I found myself nevertheless most perplexed by the fact that Max was wearing his eyeglasses, and that the lenses were distractingly crooked upon his brow. Resisting the impulse to readjust the glasses, I briskly walked past to the back halls, looking for somebody to interview.

Soon enough I was greeted by members of Max's family. Pleasantries were exchanged, and a number of comments made about my youth and calling. "Are you Robby?" asked one endearing niece from Fort Wayne.

"No," I replied innocently. "I'm Ben."

"I know that," she said, seemingly baffled. "But aren't you the *robby*?"

"Oh, the *rabbi*? Yes! I mean, yes, I am the rabbi here, and my name is Ben." The others in the anteroom where we had assembled looked at me gravely. Meanwhile, I had a problem: Max was lying out there, complete with eyewear, in an open casket. The open box not only distressed me personally, but the display was generally against Jewish tradition in the first place. Beyond that, the funeral home had positioned the dais directly above the lectern; I would be eulogizing poor Max while he stared up at me with corrected 20/20 vision. This was not going to work.

I began to explain to the gathering of relatives about the Jewish sensibility on closed coffins. It was to no avail, that warm afternoon in Wabash. Though Jews, these Hoosiers lived in a Christian world and could not relate to my more intense, urban Jewish context. Said one of them about my request that the casket be closed, "That's not the way we do things around here."

I suggested that the family retire to another room and think things over. I felt adamant about closing the casket and was actually quite upset and unnerved. Now, the funeral director, tall, throaty, Dante-esque, walked in on my brooding.

"Rabbi," he said, "the family wishes to learn about your fee."

My fee? I honestly had not considered the issue. I was still the idealistic student. "I don't have a fee," I responded. "I only want to help."

"You really ought to reconsider. The family is proud and genuinely wishes to present you with an honorarium for your service today."

I thought about it. Maybe I could take care of two issues with one bold stroke. I asked the looming director: "Have they decided what they are going to do about closing the casket?"

"Well," the gentleman sniffed, "they cannot make up their minds. Of course, we will do whatever they want, or you request."

"I'll tell you what," I said. "Tell the family that my fee is seventy-five dollars if the casket is open and fifty dollars if the casket is closed."

The lumps on the undertaker's neck appeared to pop. "I beg your pardon?"

"That's right," I said. "Go ahead and quote my prices."

"Well, all right." He turned, like a lanky flagpole and marched out. A moment later, I heard a sound. *SLAM!* It was metal against metal. The casket was clamped shut. Then the funeral director walked back into the anteroom, presented me with five very crisp ten-dollar bills and showed me into the chapel. Things were going to be okay, dear Max.

Mr. President, what is God telling you now?

October 27, 2008

It is generally understood that George W. Bush, evidently a decent-hearted, healthfully ambitious man, scion of an imperial American family, did not really know what to do with his life until he experienced a socio-political epiphany. It is hard to dismiss the steadfastness of his faith, nor the courageous will he has maintained in the matter of his alcoholism.

In spite of Oliver Stone's gratuitous attempt in the movie W to impute all of the president's angst to his supposedly thorny relationship with his father, the younger Bush has to be regarded as man of many complexities. One of these is his spirituality—it is no secret that he believes that God chose him to preside over the generically named "war on terror." Therefore, on one level, Mr. Bush is no different in depiction than the Hebrews of the Bible, who are described as "a stiff-necked people." It is also noteworthy that the entire generation of the old Hebrews had to finally give way to a new generation of young leadership, unfettered by old habits and dark convictions, and ready to adapt to the reality of a new world.

This is a faith and life column; I will not dabble in politics (although some politicians now regularly co-opt religion). There has to be a certain loneliness for the once buoyant George Bush. He concludes his eight years as president quite excoriated in public opinion—his own party eschews him, people regard his vice president as a constitutional thug, the wars he launched have been inconclusive at best, an American city drowned under his watch, and we are now in the throes of a financial meltdown and a mountainous deficit.

Mr. Bush's face is a mask when it needs to reveal contrition. No sarcasm is even hinted here when I ask, what is God telling the president now? Surely, Mr. Bush, who drew upon his theology to rationalize the US invasion of Iraq, who is stuck on convictions that strain even his most ardent apologists, still supplicates to God. Because my own tradition teaches me that we are all unequivocally the children of God, I hope that George W. Bush enjoys the benefit of divine compassion.

The president, like most people, likes to be popular, and he surely wants an honorable legacy. He sent more than 4000 American youngsters to their deaths in an invasion that history will judge critically and which very few folks regard as having in any way mitigated the force of terrorists. How do he and God converse about that, and about the scores of thousands of Americans who are maimed, burned, blinded, or broken because of their war wounds and traumas? How to soften the built-in mockery that comes with the very mention of this president, the scorn, the dismissal of his intellect, his blind eye to the corrosive effects of sanctioned torture on the national soul?

It might be George W. Bush's greatest accomplishment, then: Teach us how to pray, Mr. President, to *really* pray—because we've all been lonely and we've *needed* to pray. We'd be more comfortable with you, and you with us, if your face showed us your pain.

If Noah were running for Congress...
October 29, 2008

Opinion was mixed about Noah, the fellow who built the ark, even before he became a candidate. In the first place, he was recorded in the Bible as being "the most righteous in his generation." That's either saying a whole lot or very little.

This was the generation that was so miserable, so corrupt, so utterly brutal that God made the painful decision to wipe away the earth with a flood. There wasn't one redeeming quality in that global heap of human squalor—and Noah's the *best* one? That may not say a whole lot about the man, other than the fact that he stood out among a bunch of complete derelicts. Come to think of it, this may make him an outstanding candidate for the current Congress.

Noah had no natural ethnic following for the tracking polls to evaluate. He was neither a Jew nor a Christian—this was before either religion had developed. Basically, Noah was a pagan that God chose for God's own reasons. So, since we don't have any faith issues that would be fair game, and since he *did* do what God told him to do (construct the ark), Noah probably pulls ahead in this general category as well.

On the other hand, the Bible indicates that Noah was out there for many years, in the open, visible and available for CNN or Fox News interviews, building the ark. At no time, even as curiosity seekers looked on, and likely asked him, "Say, fella, what are you doing and why?" did Noah mention the looming calamity. He didn't even try to convert any of the riff-raff to mend their ways and thus avert the coming flood. Politically correct—probably another plus for the busy man.

But wait: When God apprised Noah that "the end of flesh was coming," and instructed him to build an ark, there's no record of Noah even protesting. Nothing like, *"What do you mean you're going to destroy the earth?"* Basically, what he said was, "OK, what are the measurements you'd prefer for the structure, God?" Abraham would argue with God when God announced the imminent demolition of two wretched cities—Sodom and Gomorrah—just in case there were a few good people to be found. Moses would argue with God when God told him atop Sinai that the people below had constructed a Golden Calf and would be annihilated. "Forget it, God," was Moses' basic response. And then, appealing to public opinion, he added: "What will the Egyptians say?" Men and women throughout the Bible fight for humanity, from Moses to Deborah to Jesus.

So it seems that Noah didn't make any controversial statements and that he followed the party line. Shoo-in.

'The annihilation of the Jews is one of the most splendid blessings'
October 30, 2008

The Islamic preacher, a leader of Hamas, actually declared: "The annihilation of the Jews in Palestine is one of the most splendid blessings." He prefaced this statement, made recently, with the following invocation: "The blessing of Palestine is dependent upon the annihilation of the pit of global corruption in it. When the head of the serpent of corruption is cut off here in Palestine, and its octopus tentacles are severed throughout the world, the real blessing will come."

That "serpent," as it were, is the successful presence of seven million Israelis thriving in a democracy for some 60 years and achieving egalitarian milestones, from a contained, disciplined people's army to the Middle East's own rendition of Silicon Valley. The Arabs refined suicide bombing, the Israelis pioneered the cellular phone, desalination, and voice Internet.

Tel Aviv went from a sand dune to a world-class cosmopolitan center of culture and technology; Beirut, once so glamorous and trendy, is defaced and scarred by internecine Arab violence and is run not by the Lebanese government but by the Hezbollah international terror syndicate. Woe unto the children of both sides—especially when clergymen invoke murder.

How do Israeli families—Rachel the teacher, Joseph the plumber, Debbie the schoolteacher, David the kindergartener—cope with this unrelenting genocidal contempt? It spawns not from the mainstream Palestinian community, the moms and dads trying also to keep their families fed and educated, safe and content, under the same century-long siege of hate, but from the men who are actually ordained as God's preachers and teachers.

Let me say, as a native of Israel, with some four generations in the land, and a wide spectrum of political beliefs (some of it unacceptably contemptuous of Arab life), that I have heard—and been pained—by pejorative talk and behavior directed against the indigenous Palestinian Arab community. But my native connections in the land compel me to inform the concerned reader that the vast majority of Israelis, exhausted and jaded by all this war-making and terrorism, *want peace.*

All you have to do is listen to contemporary Israeli pop music, read Israeli newspapers, marvel at Israeli medical and cultural creativity, and *know* that the people of Israel—the mailmen, the CEOs, the nurses, the street-pavers, and the disc jockeys, the army reservists who fill the Peace Now rallies—and you will know the heart of this moxie-state is in education, not propaganda; in movies, not militia; in outreach, not genocide.

It's hard to be so hated, especially when you just want your kids to walk safely to school, enjoy summer camp, and travel abroad without being pariahs with passports. And what have the extremist clerics of Islam—who did more killing on 9/11 in the US than in 60 years of aggregate terror against Israelis—really accomplished for Palestinian kids?

A child taught to hate without limits will never have a country with borders.

As October gave way to the colder winds and bare trees of November, a war with Hamas lay in store for Israel. Election Day in the United States pointed to a convincing and landmark victory for Senator Barack Obama and his running mate, Senator Joe Biden, over Senator John McCain and the ultimately controversial Alaska Governor Sarah Palin. Democracy would turn over peacefully in America, even as the economy plummeted beyond any recollection since the Great Depression.

But from India to Iraq and back to the Holy Land, democracy was bloodied by the armaments of terrorism. The Jewish community, always sensitive to the horror-legacy of the Holocaust, was feeling both threatened and feisty.

Thank you sir, call me a Jew
October 31, 2008

I'd rather be writing more about biblical characters who should be elected to Congress. However, somebody wrote me a nasty letter recently after something I published in this paper. *"You wrote that because you're a Jew,"* spouted my critic.

To this branding, I say, Thank you! Thank you!

Thank you for attributing to me the greatest possible ethnic compliment. Call me a Jew, and I shall be satisfied and grateful. I am so proud to be of a lineage and a people who have survived and even transcended the greatest and most unrelenting challenges ever known to any cultural group in the history of human life.

We survived Hitler, and we will survive Hamas, Hizbollah, Bin Laden and that crazy fellow in Iran. On the other hand, and in the category of hope, we produced Jesus, the greatest beacon-hero for more people of all time.

Against religious oppression, we lit the lights of Hanukkah and outshone Greek Hellenism. We wrote the texts of rabbinic Judaism and outwitted the Roman Empire. Rome is archaeology, Israel has a space program. We made Judaism portable and sprung from the clutches of the Inquisition of Spain, the pogroms of Russia and Poland, the massacres of England, the genocides of Germany, France, Latvia, and the Pale. We have always defeated brutality with the power of ideas.

We created a national Jewish homeland after Europe devoured six million of us—including nearly two million children—in fire, gas, starvation, and unimaginable bestiality. To this day, we plant trees for and honor the Righteous Gentiles who hid, protected, and died for us.

To rescue our beleaguered brethren elsewhere, we sent "magic carpets" to Yemen, Ethiopia, caravans of relief to the Arab lands, prayer books and matzos to the old Soviet Union. In a daring mission to retrieve skyjacked hostages—a rescue operation that electrified the United States on July 4, 1976—we airlifted the Star of David to Entebbe and stymied the archetypal tyrant Idi Amin.

Overcoming ingrained bigotry, we now send the stars of our American Jewish youth to every university and into every corporate hall in this country and we send our bright and ambitious former youth group presidents to Congress.

We marched with Martin Luther King, Jr., in numbers out of proportion to our actual demographics. We spilled blood in the Civil Rights Movement and some of our rabbis will not stand quiet now when they see economic and social injustice even in the state of Israel.

Call me a Jew. I like living in a people who see wrong and try to right it, see trouble and figure out how to relieve it, see life and choose to live it.

November, 2008

At Thanksgiving, there are no politics in religion.
There is only one table set for God.

McCain could not claim a moral connection to civil rights
November 4, 2008

"Boy, he has some stones," a young woman was heard to declare as Sen. John McCain stood on the balcony outside Room 306 at the Lorraine Motel in Memphis last April 4. It was raining, and umbrellas obscured the view of the presidential candidate and an initial series of boos made it hard to hear. In short, the scene was murky.

It was the 40th anniversary of the assassination of Dr. Martin Luther King, Jr. at that very spot. McCain had come there, on that historic day, to apologize for something. To be fair, this could not have been easy. But it could have been easily avoided. As an Arizona senator, he had voted in 1983 *against* the establishment of the federal holiday commemorating the birthday of Martin Luther King. Martin Luther King Day came into being regardless—under the signature, ironically—of President Ronald Reagan.

But Arizona's incongruous dissent remained a political blister for years, until the state finally joined the nation in honoring the slain moral leader in special legislation. The state passed the holiday into law in 1992 after suffering an extended tourist boycott. John McCain never apologized for his vote—and the attendant insensitivity—until he became the presumptive Republican nominee for president in 2008.

Millions of people are voting for John McCain today, and they have a variety of good reasons for doing so—above all, their freedom of choice as Americans. But it might be hard to find anyone choosing to vote for McCain because he has a spiritual connection with the American Civil Rights movement—our national story of faith, blood, and redemption. Ironically, both McCain's opponent for the presidency and his own running mate are on the national ballot today *because* of the freedom campaigns heralded so bravely and eloquently by Dr. Martin Luther King, Jr. Why did it take so long for your soul to sing, Senator?

'But thank God we ain't what we was'
November 5, 2008

"We have a long way to go before the problem is solved," declared Martin Luther King in the quaint and stately St. Paul's Episcopal Church of comfortable white folks in Cleveland Heights, Ohio, on May 14, 1963. And then he quoted the words of "an old Negro slave preacher":

"Lord, we ain't what we want to be; we ain't what we ought to be; we ain't what we gonna be; but thank God we ain't what we was."

If the dead live in any way, Dr. King is sighing in heaven this morning. It's one thing to read history, it's another thing to recall history, it's the most amazing thing to actually be alive in a moment of history.

We will all look at each differently today, black and white. Old grizzly black men, their scars of degradation leathered permanently into their skin, their heads shaking a bit in disbelief, will feel a spring in their step. Black grandmothers will hold their backs up a little straighter and try to wipe their stained eyes dry. White folks who swore it wouldn't happen will adjust their necks a bit. White folks who swore it couldn't happen will tell their children and grandchildren—we will remember, almost incongruously, the day the president was shot in Dallas, the evening the preacher fell in Memphis, the midnight that Bobby, once "our last hope," lay in his own blood and we almost weren't surprised. We will hear the echoes of "I may not get there with you…"

A whole lot of things are as unsolved this morning as they were yesterday. But no problem in this remarkably progressive and blessed America will ever be dismissed as black and white again.

And we can almost hear the proud teacher of social studies, African-American, old enough to remember, young enough to dream, praying to herself as she enters the classroom for a new day: *God keep the president safe.* Amen.

McCain, at last, releases demons along with Dems

November 6, 2008

In the end, what made so many people, including some Republicans, uncomfortable with John McCain had something to do with the sense of his tortured soul. Yes—he couldn't have defeated the national gloom that had settled in, the dark shadow of inexplicable war, the hunger for literate leadership, the feeling of lost trust, the bad faith of the axis of greed: business, oil, jingoism.

"Country first" is what John McCain truly feels, but he forgot that so do most of us. He actually didn't look at ease with the sloganeering because no man, unless he's a malcontent—which McCain is not—could possibly believe that only a certain segment of the nation actually takes America into its spirit.

The thousands of sweet young men and women who have given their lives—or their futures—to the Iraq expedition are neither Democrats nor Republicans. They are kids who have generally volunteered and they are white and black and brown and they speak a variety of languages and they missed their mothers before they were blown up and they longed for the sizzle of hot meat in their kitchens and the familiar light of their bedrooms and the voices of their friends before they died, country first.

I don't believe that John McCain, who embodies public service and really had not been a slave to his party indoctrination, could have looked like a man who sleeps with porcupines while offering his almost unendurable mantras of "reformer" and "maverick" and "I have scars to prove it," if that was really him. I don't believe that a man who suffered the kind of long incarceration that he did in North Vietnam could not have learned things that the rest of us couldn't even begin to imagine.

Demons possessed this fighting man who had *survived*, literally and politically, in his lifetime by relying on his impulse. Demons sent him, painfully disingenuous, to speak at the churches of those who once conspired with Satan to dishonor McCain's own character and soul. De-

mons   tricked him into breathlessly selecting a charming but desperately unprepared woman to potentially succeed him in office, thus
confusing a majority of his countrymen (ultimately) and putting his
running mate into a situation that strained her own legitimacy. It wasn't
fair to her, and it didn't make sense to a lot of us who want to trust our
country again, and make it part of our personal creeds.

And yet: As stunning as was his defeat, this was how gracious his
response to his former opponent and to this nation was on Tuesday
night. One had to be blind not to see the genuine anguish in John
McCain's face as he adamantly extended his war-damaged arms to stop
the initial booing that ensued upon his concession. He no longer wanted
the anger, the self-righteousness, the patriotic elitism. He wanted
peace. So vanished the demons and the country at last came first.

McCain defeat also lifted Vietnam from our souls

November 7, 2008

The election results, the third consecutive defeat of a Vietnam veteran running for president, also ended our national psyche-connection to the Vietnam War, which dragged on from 1963 to 1975. Al Gore, John Kerry, and John McCain all served in and survived the conflict; Gore did not play it up excessively, Kerry was "swift-boated" by it, and McCain was talking to a cascade of young voters who didn't understand it—or him.

It is impossible for a middle-aged male like myself, whose high school and college years were consumed by that snake-like conflict, and its demoralization of American society, not to notice that McCain's unspeakable experience in Indochina, particularly as a POW, was given due notice by the electorate and then dismissed, along with his "scars."

The national soul, which will always pay homage to the veterans of World War II (with good reason), nonetheless has brought its closure to the tragically misguided and polarizing conflict in Vietnam. This is at the same time, ironically, that the military has never enjoyed more respect and prestige. John McCain was brave—no doubt about that. But the war he survived was not noble, nor comprehensible, nor won. We have voted around it now in three presidential elections.

The trauma of that war, with its napalm, savagery, and corruption, as well as the ravaging of the Vietnamese people and the Indochinese landscape, wove its way into the psyches and lives of young people in the 1960's. The atmosphere in our nation was so poisonous from it that when Dr. Martin Luther King, Jr. stood up in 1967 to condemn it, he was excoriated and cut off from contact with his former civil rights partner, President Lyndon B. Johnson.

We young men were traumatized by the war, which was broadcast live on the nightly news—the first time a war "came into our living rooms." We were experimenting with sex and cigarettes and alcohol, we were reckless with drugs, we were fantasizing about the girls' hot pants and the way they smelled and felt up close, but we were distracted by the images of body bags and jungle infernos and POWs and the terrifying possibilities that lay in store for us once we graduated from high school and student deferments were no longer an escape. We didn't know it then, but the war was being fought by black boys in disproportionate numbers—an accounting that came later.

Perhaps one of the key innocent failures of naval test pilot and former prisoner of war John McCain was that he has never left behind a war that the rest of forgot a long time ago.

When a man conquered death and saw paradise
November 8, 2008

Forty years ago, when Barack Obama was seven, Rev. Martin Luther King, Jr., stood up on a rainy night in Memphis, exhausted, scared, and utterly prophetic. He "preached the fear of death out of himself," said a number of those present, and gave a Mosaic vision of "the Promised Land." He was killed the next day, just as he took in some fresh evening air and was remembering a hymn a particularly loved. His closing crescendo at the Mason Temple began with this dirge:

"And then I got into Memphis. And some began to say the threats, or talk about the threats that were out. What would happen to me from some of our sick white brothers?"

Then, the final 132 words of his last public address, which I see as actual rhapsody, in 17 consecutive declarations of pure prayer. For those final few moments and 132 words, MLK was suspended somewhere between earth and heaven, and he envisioned the 40 years of wandering that have come to an end, now:

1) Well, I don't know what will happen now.

2) We've got some difficult days ahead.

3) But it really doesn't matter with me now, because I've been to the mountaintop.

4) And I don't mind.

5) Like anybody, I would like to live a long life.

6) Longevity has its place.

7) But I'm not concerned about that now.

8) I just want to do God's will.

9) And He's allowed me to go up to the mountain.

10) And I've looked over.

11) And I've seen the Promised Land.

12) I may not get there with you.

13) But I want you to know tonight, that we, as a people, will get to the promised land!

14) And so I'm happy, tonight.
15) I'm not worried about anything.
16) I'm not fearing any man!
17) Mine eyes have seen the glory of the coming of the Lord!!

Why do so many evangelical teens get pregnant?

November 10, 2008

Ironically, so many right-wing fundamentalists expressed support for Sarah Palin and her family when it was announced that her unwed 17-year-old daughter Bristol was pregnant, which had little to do with ideology. It was more likely based on the fact that **teenage pregnancy** is, frankly, wide-spread among **evangelicals.**

The community deserves credit for demonstrating empathy and care for one another, along with the attendant righteousness and rationalization.

Quoted in the *National Review* this fall, the leader of evangelical out-reach for McCain-Palin stated: "There hasn't been one evangelical family that hasn't gone through some sort of situation." That individual, according to published reports, indicated that it was her own "crisis pregnancy" that thrust her into the evangelical circle.

There is a government agency that studies adolescent welfare called Add Health; it began to study adolescent life in 1994. It has worked with nearly 100,000 teens and their families in researching social and medical risk factors that young people face—the largest such examination ever. Add Health reports that evangelical teens are more sexually active than mainline Protestants, Mormons, and Jews. Apparently, evangelical Protestant teens are decidedly less likely to use contraceptives than kids from other cultural groups. This may stem from a belief system, but the result is still a wave of premarital pregnancy in this community.

Margaret Talbot, a senior fellow at the New America Foundation, has recently written in *The New Yorker* about "Red Sex, Blue Sex." She states the "The 'sexual debut' of an evangelical girl typically occurs just after she turns sixteen." She reports that a number of social scientists and family scholars have taken up this serious and troublesome social pattern that has obvious ramifications for a lot of good young women, their boyfriends or sexual partners, and the families involved.

Ms. Talbot cites the published and "startling" research of sociologist Mark Regnerus of the University of Texas—Austin: "Regnerus argues that religion is a good indicator of attitudes toward sex, but a poor one of sexual behavior, and that the gap is especially wide among teenagers who identify themselves as evangelical."

These facts and findings can be viewed as partisan, which would be such a waste of time. The real issue is the well-being and sanity of all these promising young women, their premature thrust into the complex realm of motherhood, the role of the kid-fathers, and what our already beleaguered health and social welfare systems can possibly do to accommodate the situation.

Sex education and abstinence can go hand-in-hand, rather than be viewed as necessarily adversarial socio-theological positions. And the issue of teen pregnancy is hardly confined to evangelicals. But, as it turns out, a good place to learn about the effects of this family crucible is within a community that so proudly espouses family values. As one evangelical father with a pregnant daughter was quoted as lamenting: "(It's) a problem—a major, major problem that everybody's just shoving under the rug."

'Pardon me, ma'am, but I need to be kissed'

November 11, 2008

Armistice Day, November 11, 1918, now known as Veterans' Day, originally marked the end of the First World War. It was enshrined with the end of WW II in 1945. The absolute joy and relief that swept the free world was perhaps captured no better than with the iconic photograph of a US sailor impulsively kissing a passing nurse in a festive Times Square. The dream shot occurred on V-J ('Victory in Japan') Day, August 14, 1945.

It was War meeting Love, it was America—which rescued Europe from the Nazis—reveling in the sensation of being *Home*.

The renowned snapshot was taken by photojournalist Alfred Eisenstaedt, who had ironically once photographed Adolf Hitler meeting with the Italian fascist dictator, Benito Mussolini. A German-born Jew, Eisenstaedt fortuitously fled the Third Reich with his camera and his life in 1935. He settled in New York City and began an illustrious career with *Life* magazine. His photos include Marilyn Monroe, Ernest Hemingway, Sophia Loren, and, near the end of his life, President Bill Clinton and family.

What an irony that a creative Jew, born in Prussia, took the photograph that came to symbolize the homecoming of **America's extraordinary servicemen and women** from the most dangerous and genocidal conflict in history. Much of Eisenstaedt's family was wiped out in the European extermination of 6 million Jews, along with another 6 million non-Aryans, gypsies, homosexuals, blacks, Catholic priests, and countless brave Christians who stood up against Hitler in any way. The United States lost 350,000 soldiers, the Russians lost 20 million people—in all, some *50 million people* perished on this planet, the vast majority of them civilians, and so, so many of them little children.

However difficult and challenging the world is today, we have already survived something that is unspeakably huge, and military historians know that the Allied victory over the Axis of Germany and Japan—a global conflagration that was about race as it was about anything else—was accomplished by a razor-thin margin. Though engaged in two regional wars today, Americans don't know—have no concept—about what civilian sacrifice, rationing, women replacing men in the infrastructure—are all about.

Today we thank the veterans of our military. We also salute those from the Korean War—the one everyone forgets. We continue to salve the wounds of our Vietnam veterans who were shamelessly humiliated and denied benefits and employment upon returning from a war they never conceived. We pray for our men and women in uniform in Iraq and Afghanistan and this has nothing to do with politics.

America, flawed, depressed, confused right now, is a survival kit nevertheless. May every sailor come home to a kiss.

A little humility, Gov. Palin

November 12, 2008

In contrast to the tempered demeanor of Barack Obama, the eloquent graciousness of John McCain, and the sentimental contrition of George W. Bush, Sarah Palin has seized the moment and is completely unplugged. The vice-presidential candidate who barely spoke to reporters in any spontaneous situation, who remained safely distant from political analysis or historical dissertation, is suddenly in physical pursuit of reporters, talk show appearances, and impromptu discourse.

She is inveighing against her detractors, from even within her own political party and campaign, she is calling some of her critics "jerks," and she is whining about the treatment she supposedly received from the media—the latter being the exact group that has assisted her meteoric ascent from obscurity to possible leadership of the Republican Party. In all of this bellicosity, her ally has not been her former running mate or the English language.

While the nation, including many citizens who voted for John McCain and Sarah Palin, reflects on the historic election of a black man to the White House, and looks ahead to economic reprieve and the return of our brave servicemen and women from two wars, Governor Palin remains embroiled in defense of her wardrobe, her qualifications, and her not-subtle ambitions for 2012 or 2016 or maybe even a talk show somewhere in between.

I admire the teaching of Jesus: "Take my yoke upon you and learn from me, for I am gentle and humble in heart, and you will find rest for your souls." (Matthew 11:29). Meanwhile, the hallmark and enduring characteristic of Moses was his complete meekness—in spite of vaunted fame and serious public criticism. Jesus took care of the poor and spiritually disenfranchised; Moses lifted a people from slavery to dignity. Sarah Palin might think about her deep faith and refocus now on the people in Alaska who elected her to govern them, not to use them.

Those who would truly lead us are men and women who are given to judgment and discipline. We seemed to have thrown out skin color and gender in 2008 and instead looked into the souls of our candidates. We have real problems, this beloved nation of ours. Automotive icons are falling, along with banks and bridges and schools. We need to think, while taking hold of the Judeo-Christian creed of self-control and thoughtfulness.

Dear Governor, I can see the moon from my house, but that doesn't make me an astronaut. On my good days, when my ego is in check, I see the moon or the sun or even the White House, and what I see is how small I am.

Straight from the White House: America's new holiday card

November 13, 2008

As our president-elect oversees the transition, a lot of folks are happily adjusting to new images more in keeping with the very ethics of Thanksgiving, Hanukkah, and Christmas. There was the retiring white president and his wife, scion of blue blood and Texas, warmly inviting the new president, Kenyan-Hawaiian, and his wife to tour the not-so-blanched White House anymore.

This magnificent irony was on my mind when I spoke to one of my adolescent classmates from back in 1968, just after Barack Obama handily won the presidency.

We had endured so much together, as 15-year-olds that year, 1968, including the assassinations, the Vietnam bloodshed, the urban riots, the explosive Democratic convention in Chicago that—minus the assassinated Sen. Robert F. Kennedy—nominated the party standard-bearer, Vice President Hubert Humphrey. We had walked to an urban high school day in and day out, both exhilarated and afraid, as our nation recoiled in conflict and the one thing we could have never imagined in the spring of 1968, as Dr. King was buried in Atlanta and Bobby Kennedy next to his brother in Arlington, Va., was that lightning would appear within our lifetimes and that a black man would decisively win the White House.

We remembered that other breathtaking Christmas image—when the three astronauts of Apollo 8 circled the moon, sent us back the first-ever images of a pristine blue earth, and crowned that bitter year with some genuine healing prayer from above.

"Who would have thought?" My old buddy exclaimed. We were two middle-aged men on the telephone, pondering something unimaginable 40 years ago when, within eight weeks, we lost our two signal heroes that summer, MLK and RFK.

My friend's sentiment was palpable, and I heard the painful cry of history being released, like a millstone, across the phone lines. Suddenly, it wasn't all in vain—the shootings of Medgar Evers, Malcolm X, Dr. King, and so many others whose names are only known to God. Suddenly, it wasn't about the superficial and financially driven plethora of brand-name black athletes selling deodorants, cars, sneakers, beer, and pension portfolios on television. It wasn't window dressing or affirmative action or quota-filling. It was real, thrilling and, though it was a political campaign, it ultimately was dignified. It smacked of reconciliation; it's the bellwether of an uncommon festival.

It also proved that in America, 40 years after the moon was first beamed into our homes, lightning flashed across the plains and the mountains with the incandescence of hope. Barack Obama was not really the first one to declare, "Yes, we can." But he was first one to say it, with black skin, and to win the tentative rewriting of American holiday dreams.

Love was the festival before the holiday became a chore

November 14, 2008

An old story, drawn from the Talmud, tells of a Roman matron who approached a sage and asked: "In how many days did God create the universe?" The Romans were in control of ancient Judea then and were often depicted in Jewish sources as gaining insight from rabbinic authorities. The sage responded: "God created the universe in six days.

"Well then," the Roman lady persisted. "What's he been doing since then?"

The sage responded without hesitation: "He's been creating love."

Now that the holidays are approaching, and there is stress, and mercantilism, and a bad economy, and so many lists, menus, and requirements: How goes it for you with your partner in love? Can any material things you buy or accumulate possibly equal the value of that love? And when January comes, and with it the cold winds of debt and some depression, will the love you feel add or subtract from your emotional accounting?

Now—before the rush, before the tensions and aggravations that invariably defile Christmas and even compromise little Hanukkah—now is the time to consider the one you love. Is there any greater gift than this? Can it be measured in credit card points or frequent flier miles? Does it even require wrapping? Issac Bashevis Singer wrote that human love is "a sensation no scientist has named, which inflames the heart and marrow with wantonness and a desire that cannot be withstood."

You don't have to believe in God to believe that the way you love someone is divine. Once you remember this, you've got Thanksgiving cooked, Hanukkah freed, and Christmas redeemed. And since these pressured holidays, with their pretense and their indulgence, their defiance of spirituality in favor of acquisition, are so at odds with the meaning of love, this is the time to consider how much your beloved means to you.

Love is an indication of godliness. It was with this inexplicable feeling, this unique yearning that one human being can develop for another, this song to the sky that drives us to absolutely require another person's presence in our own soul, this sometimes maddening contract between two hearts, that God left behind the ingredients for the unfolding creation known as human life. God created the world, but people are creating it. God makes rain, but people make love. Before you buy, remember to embrace.

Remember when your net worth was not about money?

November 15, 2008

The bride and groom walked down the aisle practically intertwined. Their arms were locked together; they actually stumbled down the runway, tripping over each other's feet and bumping into each other's trembling shoulders. Their cheeks touched, their faces rubbed, their fingers groped over each other's knuckles. These two were in desperate need of one another. The tall candles that lined the aisle dimmed in contrast to this shared human incandescence.

Younger people gazed upon this, their breath stopped short by the physical appearance of romance in the hall. The scene gave credence to their innocent speculations on love. Middle-aged couples smiled knowingly, recalling the headier days of their youth, when love was more of a feeling and less of a noble yet practical condition. Widows felt their hearts bitten by something bittersweet yet reassuring. Many in the room spoke to themselves; a soft swell of silent prayers filled the air above the flowers, the lights, the wedding canopy itself.

For this moment, there were no issues to ponder, no budgets to consider, no career goals to reconcile, no religious partitions to negotiate. All the parents were sympathetic in-laws, all the relatives were one household, all the friends were supportive voices. The community sighed with relief, the nation was calm, the world was at peace. Love drifted through the room; not a few present would have conceded that God had been busy creating something.

The rabbinic commentary on the biblical Song of Songs tells us: "When a man is young, he sings about love. When he matures, he speaks pragmatic proverbs. When he grows old, he speaks about the vanity of things." Love is an evolution of experience; on this night, the groom was a young man singing of love.

Couples of all persuasions, creeds, and genders: Love is the only dividend and the "interest" rate adds to the equation rather than compounds. The holidays approach: Buy less, sing more, and you will notice the gifts you won't return.

Why in the world would Sunday be Sabbath?
November 16, 2008

A lot of folks ask me this, most often in genuine curiosity, and because the Hebrew Scripture leaves no doubt that the Sabbath was Saturday—the *seventh* day of the week. "And on the seventh day God rested," we all read in Genesis; there's just no qualm about that, after God made the first human beings on the sixth day, Friday.

Indeed, Jews and early Christians shared the biblical practice of the Saturday Sabbath (in fact the only Hebrew word for Saturday is *Shabbat*) in the early Christian period. This was under the supervision and inspiration of James (the brother of **Jesus**), Peter, and other disciples. According to a leading Canadian religious history compendium, the first Christians followed Mosaic traditions, including sacrifice in the Jerusalem Temple, and the Saturday Sabbath work restrictions.

Many other scriptural configurations retain the multiple of seven, including the sabbatical year of rest for farmland and soil, the 49th year of Jubilee for the manumission of slaves, and, again, the weekly respite and prayer gatherings on Saturday. In **Israel** today, Sunday remains the first day of the work week, the school week, and the resumption of bus and train operations that were suspended on Friday evenings. Of course, Christians native to the Holy Land may adjust to the secular Sunday in terms of banking and grocery shopping, but they wholeheartedly offer devotions in the historic churches of Jerusalem, Bethlehem, and Nazareth—with the full sanction and protection of the Israeli government, incidentally.

Why did **Christianity** eventually change the Sabbath to Sunday? In the first place, candidly, it had to—in order to create a distinction from Judaism, its parent religion—but foil nonetheless. But there's also significant evidence and precedent that played to this important transformation and Jews shouldn't smugly think that Christians chose Sunday simply because "Saturday was already taken."

For some four centuries after Christ, Christians lived mainly in a pagan world, and not so much among Jews. Christianity became the official religion of the Roman Empire in the 4th century, an empire that had swirled in paganism and the Persian-based Mithraism all along. Mithraism was Sunday-centered, so it was natural for Christians to follow suit. But not to be underestimated were: 1) the powerful call of the Resurrection, which occurred on Sunday, and, 2) the desire for Christians to differentiate themselves from the Jews.

The Roman government intermittently persecuted the Jews at this time; it was safer for Christianity to be considered as a separate religion rather than as a sect of Judaism. In 321 CE, while he was a pagan sun-worshiper, the Emperor Constantine declared that Sunday was to be a day of rest throughout the Roman Empire. Ultimately, it became a given, theologically, politically, socially, even from the point of view of power and control, for Christianity to formally adopt Sunday as the Sabbath. The Church Council of Laodicea ordered that religious observances were to be conducted on Sunday, not Saturday. Sunday became the new Sabbath. They ruled: *"Christians shall not Judaize and be idle on Saturday, but shall work on that day."*

The Jewish community has never challenged the Christian Sabbath (not even being in a position to) and welcomes the postmodern respect—even affection—for Jewish customs that are so integral to most Church liturgies, some sixty years after the Holocaust. Islam, which came along in the fifth century, and selected Friday, will hopefully follow suit.

Who wouldn't yearn to put a fence around a country like this?

November 17, 2008

Israel has a complicated agenda—remaining the only *bona fide* democracy in the Middle East for 60 years now, supplying the US with comprehensive antiterrorism intelligence, maintaining its capital and federal bureaucracy in Jerusalem while guaranteeing freedom of access to and security for all religious holy sites—all while protecting its citizens from rocket attacks, suicide bombings, and the declared threat of an Iranian nuclear genocide.

Israel has to be normal, while being the Holy Land.

So the Israelis, who pioneered cellular technology, laser surgery, and water desalination, decided to build a wall to keep the homicide bombers out. It's been effective, even as the US, dealing with a porous border, is building a complex fence system along the Mexican frontier.

A couple of years ago, the International Court of Justice at The Hague took up part of its day by ruling that a major portion of the barrier Israel is building between itself and the Palestinians is illegal. Palestinian extremist leaders considered it a victory; Israel considered it another day to work on the fence. Most of us Jews thought of it as another day in the European theater of anti-Semitism.

What other nation in the world—particularly an exemplary egalitarian state like Israel—would ever be asked not to build something that might stop somebody from killing a child at school or a grandmother walking home from the market? The people of Israel, who have borne the specter of this unimaginable predicament while still building their country, should be exalted for their forbearance and creativity that have continued while too many in the Arab world have wallowed in unseemly goals and dreadful accomplishments—like 9/11 and 7/7 and the suicide killings of American soldiers in Afghanistan and Iraq.

Who wouldn't want to put up a fence around such a nation? And what young soldier, male or female, wouldn't want to protect the schoolchildren and elders of this old-new land?

The fence is not ideal, and it has caused hardship to some innocent Palestinians. Israelis concede this, while clutching their children. Moreover, the *majority* of Israeli citizens overwhelmingly favor major concessions to the Palestinians just to attain the peace; the prime minister of the state has committed himself to a secure agreement with the Palestinian people that finally ends what he at last concedes has been an "occupation" and that he realizes is not in the true Jewish spirit.

Who wouldn't yearn to put a fence around such a noble and brave little holy land—unless somebody didn't understand the meaning of love?

This essay originally appeared in the
San Diego Union-Tribune.

'A broken promise in Jerusalem…'

November 18, 2008

Whenever I'm not sure about things, I close my eyes and visit Jerusalem. Its fury and passion arouse me from the doldrums—a city of seductive archways and obstinate walls, a stumbling block, a stairway to heaven.

While men and women debate its sovereignty in parliamentary halls, Jerusalem goes about its business, its stones betraying more wisdom than all the mighty warriors who've come and gone from its golden terraces.

I like to linger in Jerusalem—an undivided, if tense, city of God since 1967. It is the ultimate paradox of secularism and religiosity. It is the living argument, and it will verify whether people can live together, once and for all.

What an awesome place this city is—this amalgam of superstores, Torah academies, soccer fields, synagogues, mosques, churches, luxury hotels, sacred tunnels, traffic jams, holiday menorahs, neon lights, rabbinic courts, parliamentary buildings, Talmudic seminaries, civic license bureaus, kosher certifying agencies, army checkpoints, *mezuzah* inspectors, and metal detectors. Looking at spiritual history, it would seem, as one modern writer has asserted, that trivial encounters in the narrow streets of the Old City can determine the human condition.

A broken promise in Jerusalem, a night of romance, an act of mercy, might be studied for centuries to come as a guide to the will of the universe. I fly off to the Western Wall, physical remnant of the King David's Temple, with its protective Hasidic clans, as thick as blackberries; the Damascus Gate only a sprint away, completely trafficked by kaffiyeh-laden Arab merchants, worshipers, and soothsayers. Jerusalem, a dream in painful progress, torn from within, with timeworn blood stains practically still visible across crescent domes and ringing Christian bells and swift taxis and beleaguered mules—the ultimate paradox of Semitic spirituality and secularism.

I eat picked-dashed lamb *shwarma* at the tiny eateries of kindly Arab hosts, dousing the delicacy in thick hummus, deliciously completed by hot-sweet Turkish coffee. At night, I swap stories with fellow clergy along the chilly terrace of the most famous "YMCA" building in the world, sipping on the orange-chocolate Israeli liqueur called "Sabra."

The morning comes, and in the stillness, in the golden haze, there is this fleeting illusion that Jerusalem has fulfilled all of its broken promises and satisfied the meaning of its name, *city of peace*. And still I return, because my prayers are never as dense as in these stony, stubborn hills, in these arched, narrow walkways of hope.

This old ballplayer understands life better than most

November 19, 2008

Jack Aker, a name known to aficionados of the national pastime, is something of a legend. But if his baseball card could talk, you'd hear a lot more than breezy play-by-play. Here's a guy who made more appearances (495) as a relief pitcher than anybody in his time, but found himself taken out of the game quite before he expected. Like anybody suddenly not doing the thing we've been doing forever, Jack found himself looking down the abyss—he was tearful, anxious, and despondent.

Baseball players are real people, in spite of the hype we impose on them, and their souls hurt, their spirits droop, just like all hard-working Americans.

Jack won the *Sporting News* "Fireman of the Year" award in 1966 and played for the Kansas City and then Oakland Athletics, the Seattle Pilots, New York Yankees, Chicago Cubs, Atlanta Braves, and New York Mets. When I met him some years ago, he was pitching coach of the Cleveland Indians; I caught my breath short, extending and receiving hands of friendship with a living and breathing major leaguer who was on a first-name basis with such stars as Phil Niekro and Tom Seaver.

I saw him at his tallest. Arriving on the green natural field before game time, Jack came for me, in full regalia—snappy cap and shimmering team jacket. He walked across fresh, chalky baselines with a certain, lanky royalty. There were the first faint smells of popcorn and beer from the bowels of the old stadium as the coach escorted me into the clubhouse.

Jack took me into a comfortably large room filled with open booths that served as repositories for the players. "Here," he declared, "we meet and discuss the game plan." Like a knothole sentry, he walked past the colognes and hair dryers of the bath area towards a large bin containing thick, polished baseball bats. He said, somberly: "Nobody can touch a man's bat. You see, Ben, they are numbered according to his uniform number. The bat is a very personal matter to a guy. Nobody can touch it."

I understood what a sacrilege was and I shook my head in awe of power and success.

A little over a year later, following a season of fallen expectations and profits, Jack (and the team manager) were both summarily dismissed from their positions. Now, this same Jack, record-holder, my invincible hero, sat in the front of my automobile, shoulders slumped, his head in his hands. We were taking a ride in the country as the venerable coach tried to sort things out.

His prestige, his income, and his self-image were suddenly as powdery as the faded chalk lines of that emerald ball field he had once ruled.

Jack was gone, the manager was gone, as well as a number of the muscular, sleek, swaggering players I had met that shining afternoon—in a different season.

A person is so much more than his baseball card, her resume, his cellular list of "contacts." Jack is doing okay, taking in his children and grandchildren, knowing well what it means to be laid off, discarded, discontinued. Maybe this old ballplayer understands America right now better than most.

This essay originally appeared in the
Cleveland Plain Dealer.

As America took in the quiet dignity and resolve of its new president-elect, Barack Obama, jobs were indeed disappearing, and the economy "tanked"—as many said or wrote. Many commented on the tremendous, if not unparalleled, burdens of office the new president was inheriting. He employed a refrain, "We have only one president at a time." In fact, he was already a kind of "acting president," as banks failed and/or merged, Congress wrestled with unfathomably lavish bailouts for Wall Street, and the Middle East was smoldering. Things were getting testy within the Catholic Church, as well.

No communion if you voted for Obama
November 20, 2008

So declared a Catholic priest in Greenville, S.C., adding that supporting the president-elect "constitutes material cooperation with intrinsic evil." The story was filed by the Associated Press on November 14, ten days after Sen. Barack Obama's convincing electoral victory and 232 years after the founding parents of this nation established the separation of church and state as national doctrine.

The AP dispatch quoted Rev. Jay Scott Newman, a son of the Blue Ridge Mountains and a former Baptist and Episcopalian, and one-time atheist. Forgetting his personal journey through choices, the priest wrote a letter to his parishioners warning them that they were putting their souls at risk if they took Holy Communion before doing penance for their vote.

The letter included the following pronouncement:

"Voting for a pro-abortion politician when a plausible pro-life alternative exists constitutes material cooperation with intrinsic evil, and those Catholics who do so place themselves outside of the full communion of Christ's Church and under the judgment of divine law. Persons in this condition should not receive Holy Communion until and unless they are reconciled to God in the Sacrament of Penance, lest they eat and drink their own condemnation."

Persons in this condition? The last time I heard something like this—and felt true anguish for good people just going about their business in a world that is so theologically hot-blooded—was when some fundamentalist rabbi in Israel declared that the genocide of the six million Jews by the Nazis was the result of Reform Judaism having been created in Germany.

I have thirty years of interfaith work to fall back on, much of it with generously enlightened and beneficent Catholic priests and sisters and theologians—many of whom carry in their hearts a deep conviction that abortion is not consistent with the notion of life. I respect them profoundly, and their religious convictions—particularly when they have enough respect for democracy not to inveigh against the republic's foundations by insinuating a connection between the secrecy of the ballot box and the privacy of one's divinity.

Father Newman is entitled (by the Constitution) to his moral outrage. But he is not entitled to impugn anyone with his contempt for freedom. This nation—the greatest experiment in democracy ever achieved in world history—was founded by Judeo-Christian men and women who were extremely sensitive to, even suspicious of, religious contravention in civil matters. Just read Jefferson or Franklin and you will discover a pretty dim view of religious practices altogether.

This is one of few American matters that is, ironically, black and white. Sadly, just as the American people concluded an historical election in peace and honor, here is an unfortunate screed that incites people to a scary gray that could ultimately lead to the flow of red.

11/22/63: JFK killed, and we were never young again

November 21, 2008

It was exactly forty-five years ago, Nov. 22, 1963 (today is the corresponding Friday), when President John F. Kennedy, 46, was slain while riding in a motorcade in Dealey Plaza, Dallas. The world stopped, the kinetic, violent, transformational 1960s truly sprung, at 12:30 PM CST, when the shots were fired from the Texas School Book Depository Building.

Television news, essentially black-and-white, thickly wired, carried forward with bright lights and sweating, nervous-lipped men, transmorphed from puberty to fullness: The dreadful dispatches were piped in by only the three networks, spoken by hushed, urgent-sounding men, about confusion and blood and crushed flowers and a young widow in Texas. There wasn't regular programming of any kind on radio or television until Tuesday, November 26, the day after the young president was laid to rest in Arlington National Cemetery.

The '60s, which began in Dallas, sprouted birth control pills, the Beatles, more assassinations, endless war and summer riots, Woodstock, and the first landing on the moon.

A wispy, eerie assassin named Lee Harvey Oswald, ex-Marine, alleged commie, Russian expatriate, came through the cathode ray of the television set with the pronged antennae and click-click channel setter. We had real demons to fear and young men to bury, starting with the chestnut-haired president and hemorrhaging into thousands and thousands of peach-fuzzed soldiers who began to die for us in the jungles and rice-paddies and fires of Vietnam.

Broadcast live on my luckless living room Zenith, a stocky, TV-gangster look-a-like named Jack Ruby thrust himself out of the grainy crowd in the Dallas police garage and fired a pistol into the sweater of Lee Harvey Oswald that very Sunday afternoon, November 24, 1963. Suddenly, the government and policemen were no longer sacrosanct as we assumed they were and nothing seemed as safe as we took for granted it would be. There was now "A Threat" out there. Violent death was abruptly an unwelcome companion in our thoughts. There was a new vulnerability; some thought of fleeing to Canada to avoid the inexplicable war in Indochina.

Race riots scorched everything the next several summers from Newark to Watts. Japanese cars and lavish bar mitzvah parties and Afros and bell-bottoms and condoms came through like the tide and my sixth-grade crushes went on to their lives and our innocent little flirtations were as distant and ethereal as the morning stars disappearing into the blazing light of a post-modernity that everyone feted but none of us really, truly welcomed.

President Kennedy, we still miss you—and how we felt before everything was scattered, like the frightened birds fleeing the ricocheting bullets of Dealey Plaza, 11/22/63.

How do you miss a parent you never really knew?

November 22, 2008

Over the years," she wrote, "I've been deeply moved by the people who've told me they wished they could feel inspired and hopeful about America the way people did when my father was president." Caroline Kennedy published these words in *The New York Times* last January (while endorsing Barack Obama for president).

But this writer is not thinking politics on this milestone November 22 — the exact 45th anniversary of the assassination of Caroline's father, President John F. Kennedy. She never knew him as an adolescent, a high school graduate, college co-ed, a bride; she can only emulate him and hear other people's memories in her emergence for some time now as a teacher, author, social activist, and, above all, the mother of three teenagers, Tatiana, Jack, and Rose. These are President Kennedy's only grandchildren.

This has to be a bitter weekend for Caroline Kennedy, who was raised and profoundly shaped by her mother, Jacqueline Kennedy Onassis (who died in 1994), has been a paragon of privacy, dignity, restraint, and literacy—even while remaining, obviously, a public figure. This is the weekend her father was buried during the most examined state funeral in American history (a funeral assembled by a government in total shock and unpreparedness), and this also is the weekend of the birthdays (both on November 25) of her brother John, Jr., who perished in a plane crash in 1999, and her uncle Senator Robert F. Kennedy—assassinated in 1968 during his own brief and haunting campaign for the presidency.

How do you remember a parent you never really knew? Do you rely on other people's narratives? These are colored by heavy layers of subjectivity, and historical annals are often tainted with self-interest or downright hostility. Caroline did have her remarkable mother for thirty years and in this garden her family tree was watered generously. But in the end, the real father, the *Dad* she has sought to understand and love, has so much been converted into an icon, a coin, a college, an aircraft carrier, an airport named JFK.

As Caroline's mother once wrote in anguish: "So now he is a legend when he would have preferred to be a man."

If you want to know something of Caroline Kennedy's soul, do read her magnificent anthology, *A Patriot's Handbook: Songs, Poems, Stories, and Speeches Celebrating the Land We Love.* Happily, Caroline grew up and allowed neither our deification nor demonization of her Dad to affect her relationship with life and with this nation. Rather, she turned to the true voices of national pride and pain, from the likes of Daniel Webster to Harper Lee to Martin Luther King to Lillian Hellman to Bob Dylan, and she lives in a place within her soul that is as true to this turbulent nation as it is to herself.

Now let every soldier look into the mirror
November 25, 2008

As the solstice holidays approach, and so many truly pray for peace—
finally, peace—the story of one fanciful soldier might be placed in every
military manual: It happened in 1948, in Jerusalem, the city of peace that
has never actually known serenity.

A sensitive young man named Gabriel Stern had arrived in Jerusalem
in the late 1930s from Germany—just eluding the Nazi gas chambers
and ovens. The narrative is shared by Tom Segev in his book, *1967*. My personal interest in Gabriel stems from his unique life story and his special
yearning: Landing from the gates of hell into a land of biblical history and
promise, he took up Middle Eastern studies at Hebrew University. His
goal was to help create reconciliation between Jews and Arabs; this was
seventy years ago, before even World War II, the Holocaust, and the post-
9/11 world in which we find ourselves.

Alas, as Israel became a state in 1948, with full UN sanction, it had to
defend itself from the coordinated invasion of several Arab armies. The
dreamer Gabriel Stern became a soldier and he found himself stationed at
a guard post in the Italian Hospital of Jerusalem's Musrara neighborhood.

But this is not about war or the reasons for it. It's about what could
transpire if every soldier experienced what happened one mystical day in
1948 to Gabriel Stern.

As Segev writes: On guard duty in the Italian Hospital, Stern "found
himself face-to-face with a man in uniform who was aiming a gun at him,
finger on the trigger. The enemy. The man was standing at the end of a
long, dimly lit corridor. Stern did not know how he had gotten there. He
felt at that moment that his life was on the line: One of them would open
fire and live. The other would die.

Stern pulled the trigger. The bullet went straight into the figure—and
shattered it into a thousand fragments of glass: it was a large mirror. Stern
had shot at himself. He never shot at anyone again."

Let every government look into the mirror before the world is a heap of
broken glass. Let every soldier lay down the gun, one by one—it's the
only way, for the love of God.

It's the one true holiday, bigger than religion
November 26, 2008

What must God think of all the arguing about religion? Thanksgiving is a day when heaven may get some relief from this concern, when Americans of all faiths sit at one spiritual table with many of the same trimmings and family customs. Thanksgiving liberates us from specific theological claims and allows us to contemplate the common creed of gratitude. In a way, it's the only pure holiday.

We celebrate Thanksgiving as a uniquely inclusive **American** moment of community faith. It is an untainted day, a blessed coda just prior to the commercial frenzy of Christmas and Hanukkah. We are all seated at the table with one God. Almost every other day of the year is tinged with religious constraints and spiritual divisiveness. This holiday mitigates the fundamentalism that seeps into too much of the great American faiths, creating a sense of exclusion that divides our children and obviates the exemplary spirit of togetherness shown by Native Americans to the new pilgrims back in 1623.

If this day offers warm bread for empty bellies and cold turkey from religious coercion, then our children are well served and our country is morally redirected.

Young people think a lot about God, and they tend to view religion with some skepticism. Perhaps they are more convinced of adult hypocrisy in this category than in almost any other. Dealing with fears that were unimaginable when we were in high school a generation or two ago, these kids are generally unimpressed with any obsessive claims that one religion may hold against another.

Tomorrow, we should talk to our children about the meaning of spiritual wholeness. They hear a lot from religious zealots in school, on television and across the Internet. Tomorrow is one of those rare days when we actually gather as families, and it is worth noting that every American family fortunate enough to have a table and some bread is pretty much saying the same prayers.

This is the shared Thanksgiving epiphany—the gospel of gratitude.

Thanksgiving allows all the religions to share inclusive spiritual nourishment. Soon enough, some of our children will return to college, the homeless will return to lonely desperation, and many of us will regress to the mercantile madness of the December holidays. Jewish parents will fret again about the proliferation of Christmas symbols and images while both **Jews and Christians** will forget to infuse the subsequent holidays with the ethical symmetry that Thanksgiving gives us for now.

Jews, remember what you feel tomorrow when you light the Hanukkah lights in a few weeks. Christians, recall Thursday's spiritual equity when you light the candles of the Advent wreath. At Thanksgiving, there are no politics in religion. There is only one table set for God.

This article is adapted from a piece originally written with Crickett Karson in the *Cleveland Plain Dealer.*

I got a second chance at life
November 27, 2008

I am so in love. It's Thanksgiving night, and we are sated and happy and grateful—and not unaware of the countless millions in our very America who remain hungry and in the dark. But what I know, above all, is that I am hopelessly in love.

The spicy aromas of brined turkey and banana bread and sweet potatoes and apple pie linger in the house as my beloved smiles in satisfaction and—hardly a servile wife—nonetheless takes delight in our savory weariness. I helped a little, but she was the chef of an exquisite meal of Americana cuisine, everything exceedingly moist and fresh and luscious, delivered in cheerful good spirits to our cadre of family, including my mother, one of my visiting out-of-town daughters, her beau, and our faithful Dalmatian who has taken in all the available scraps with aplomb. And I can't take my eyes off my wife, strong-shouldered, brisk, and impossibly pretty; the one who invented joy and compassion and high standards. Audrey is my muse, my best friend, my religion.

We celebrated our fourth wedding anniversary just last month. Leaving the children behind (my step kids are teenagers; my own two daughters are adult denizens of Chicago and New York), we slipped away to nearby Palm Desert, and, while she worked arduously during the day as a corporate executive, we partied at night and marked a milestone of romance and distinguished hard work. Her emerald eyes moist with meaning and experience, we toasted our hard times and our commitment to deal with everything—angry former spouses, ambivalent children, personal career transitions, an opinionated circle of friends, most deeply supportive, some critical—and transcended everything in the name of our incontrovertible love.

When does a second marriage, one that followed two parallel, if doomed, marriages involving children and longtime friends, nonetheless prove its integrity around the table on a Thanksgiving night? Perhaps when a man weeps with the sense that he is *actually* grateful, that none of the trappings and rituals and family winks and old generational clichés are ceremonial and perfunctory. When a glass of wine is filled with bittersweet wisdom, when a clutching of the hands under the table is the ripe trembling of a knowing and powerful connection, when an adult daughter can tell you that she believes at last that your happiness is more important—and more an entitlement—than any old grudges and resentments.

And, above all, it's when you realize that it's not because you're so smart or charming or strong. It's because you're lucky—lucky that Audrey risked so much because she thought you understood her pain and could make her hear music and only wanted to be inspired by the coming of the morning. And when you let her down, and you fell into moods, and you doubted yourself, she stayed with you, and let you find yourself even when you were too soaked in guilt and self-pity to even look.

We are here, around a table carved with fear, polished with confidence, and finished with laughter. If Thanksgiving is national, my gratitude is celestial.

And then, a storm broke out in Mumbai, India...

How do you wrap people in their prayer shawls and then kill them?
November 30, 2008

Throughout this Thanksgiving weekend, we have been deeply distressed and we have shaken our heads in shocked dismay at the ghastly blood-baths in Mumbai. It has been impossible for us to be thankful for America without taking to heart the scores of innocent victims (mostly *not* Americans or Britons, supposedly targeted) who were randomly shot up—men, women, little children—by a handful of well-disciplined sea-invading men made insane by their Islamic religious mentors.

The Jewish element of this madness has not been overlooked by the media, and it has been commented on by many sympathetic spiritual leaders in our country. The Islamic terrorists, including one surviving Mumbai attacker, have hardly been reticent about it. Jews and Israelis were specifically targeted and the horrifying slaughter of a young rabbi and his wife, among others, ensued at the Chabad House—a center for prayer, housing, social welfare, and food distribution.

According to published reports in *The New York Times* and the *Jerusalem Post*, some of the terrorists had actually rented rooms at the Chabad House in the months prior to this atrocity. They took in the hospitality and joined in the meditation while staking out the place for their assiduously planned murder rampage. Unbelievably, the assassins exacerbated the terror by wrapping their victims in their own prayer shawls before shooting them in the skulls.

The cords of death encompassed me, and the straits of the nether-world got hold upon me; I found trouble and sorrow. (Psalm 116:3)

We recited psalms in our synagogues for every sufferer—Jew, Christian, Hindu, Muslim—all innocent victims of the divine perjury that is spreading, like spiritual carcinoma, from the caves of Islamic cabalists who are warped in some kind of medieval spell.

Yet we took relief in the fact that the infant son of the murdered Rabbi Gavriel and Rivka Holtzberg was miraculously smuggled out of the

Chabad House by an employee just before the horror ensued. The little child is safely in the hands of his grandparents. His name is Moses.

This is not the first time that a baby Moses somehow survived a designated pogrom—it is the story of our beloved Moses in Egypt, set adrift by his frightened parents into the Egyptian bulrushes after Pharaoh commanded the mass murder of Jews. Who knows but that this Moses will grow up and lead us out of this wilderness?

May the memory of the dead, all God's children, be for blessing.

December, 2008

In the name of Moses, Jesus, and Mohammed,
can't we all have a real Christmas?

What do we tell our kids about these images?
December 1, 2008

In this postmodern world of Internet and 24-hour conglomerate news media outlets, there is nowhere a teenager cannot visit, no limit to his/her exposure, unmonitored on a cellular phone, to the world's horrors. A corrupt police sergeant beheads someone in Tijuana—the kid in Atlanta knows it, sees it, dreams of it. Terrorists overrun Mumbai with guns and grenades—junior high school students cope with the pictures of it, from Santa Monica to Times Square.

There has always been evil in the world; it's just that now it's broadcast live, via satellite, in high-dimension color, and hyper-repetitively—our perception of it is thereby keen and multiplied and unimaginably overbearing. If CNN and Fox and MSNBC were telecasting during World War II, there would have been even more of a general gloom in 1944 than there is in 2008 about violence and inhumanity. Even Hitler didn't have a web site; today, every bloodthirsty *mufti* has one.

Unfortunately, the omnipresence of media has emboldened Islamic terrorists and so we have a metamorphic cycle of terror and television. A kid today can revisit 9/11 at any time on her laptop, or he can, at leisure, study the autopsy photos of President John F. Kennedy's murdered body.

Years ago, my elder daughter woke up, terror-stricken, in the middle of the night. Like any youngster, she had succumbed in her dreams to the constant barrage of unspeakable images that assaulted her from television and video. Holding her and kissing her trembling head, I heard her gasp: "I'm afraid somebody is going to kidnap me and hurt me. I'm afraid somebody is going to shoot me with a gun."

How do you respond to a child in this situation? You look directly at her so that she can see the most important thing in the world: Your face. You listen to him as he pours out his emotions. Let the poison drain out. You wrap your arms around him and let him stay a good while, because very adult-like fears have turned this teenager back into a child this night. You don't depend upon a surrogate, a teacher, or a politician to comfort your offspring with the parental love and comfort only you can give.

And then ask yourself how well you really know your child—has your own preoccupation with career, power, and vanity left him or her too reliant on a cybernetic substitute for you?

Talk about the terror in India with your family *now*; CNN can get them the information but only you can provide the knowledge.

When you break the hearts of babies

December 2, 2008

When terrorists seized the Chabad House in Mumbai, nanny Sandra Samuel locked herself in a laundry room, as she tried to comprehend the situation and find a way to save herself and others. Sandra had been a longtime worker at the community house, where people routinely gathered to pray, share meals, and perform good works in the city. She specifically looked after Moshe ('Moses')—the 2-year-old curly-haired son of Rabbi Gavriel Holtzberg, 29, and his wife Rivka, 28. In the midst of gunfire and pure terror, Sandra would save the little boy, even as his parents were murdered while he watched.

According to Associated Press reports filed from Jerusalem, the nanny heard Moshe's mother screaming "Sandra, help!" Then the howling stopped, and it was still. The child had been somehow spared bullets and he sat with his pants drenched in his parents' blood.

We are all still waiting to hear from a thoughtful Islamic teacher on the rationale for this world *jihad* against babies, young parents, innocent tourists, airline passengers, embassy workers, US soldiers, Christians, Jews, Hindus, and any Muslims who happen to be in the way.

From the Associated Press: *Sandra cracked open the door of her hiding place and saw a deserted staircase. She ran up one flight and found the rabbi and his wife, covered in blood and shot to death. She snatched up the crying boy, bolted down the stairs and ran out of the building.*

My own family in Israel watched the televised memorial service for the young rabbi and his wife, which took place in a Mumbai synagogue.

From the Associated Press: *The cries of little Moshe wounded hearts..."Mommy, mommy, mommy!" he wailed, clutching a toy basketball while squirming in the arms of mourners at the synagogue.*

Afterwards, an Israeli air force jet flew Moshe, Sandra Samuel, the baby's maternal grandparents, and a few others to Tel Aviv to prepare for the burials of the young couple and the other four Israeli victims of the wanton siege in Mumbai. The toddler had never been to Israel, was now orphaned and enshrined in history, and just wanted his Mommy.

There will be serious discussions about the ultimate custody of Moshe Holtzberg. But people of faith are already forming a family circle around this little Moses and he will grow old, please God, in safety and warmth—even as he will undoubtedly retain the memories of his parents' screams and the stains of their blood.

We are all custodians of Moses and every child in this world orphaned by the current insanity. We will defeat their brutality with the power of our love. But even the biblical Moses (who also survived terror as a baby) ultimately turned the mantle over to Joshua, the general.

Israel waters its gentile trees
December 3, 2008

Sandra Samuel, an Indian woman of quiet strength and uncommon valor, never had a passport till the other day. Without fanfare and lacking any agent or public relations specialist, she did more for human life that dreadful morning in Mumbai last week than Britney Spears or Paris Hilton or Lucy Liu have accomplished in their lifetimes. Britney may have trimmed down for her birthday and gotten great photo ops, but Sandra Samuel saved an infant's life literally in the face of blazing machine guns and grim killers. She did not seek a photo.

Sandra Samuel now continues to help care for the heartbreakingly famous baby Moshe Holtzberg in Israel, after rescuing him from the terrorists who murdered his young parents, and other Jews, at the Chabad House. Her emigration from India was expedited when the Israeli government declared her one of the "Righteous Persons" and issued her immigration papers. Recipients of this honor, awarded by a special Supreme Court commission in Israel, include Oskar and Emilie Schindler, Raoul Wallenberg, and Corrie ten Boom. People and groups that receive this title have risked their lives to save others, many during the Holocaust. Sandra Samuel is evidently the first citizen of India to receive this honor.

Baby Moshe's parents, Rabbi Gavriel and Rivka Holtzberg, neither of them even 30 years old,were buried yesterday in Jerusalem's Mt. of Olives Cemetery. Under a reign of fire and having actually faced down their killers, Sandra Samuel lifted the baby from the bloody corpses of his parents and fled to safety and then a "homecoming" in Israel. Nobody who was ever a human being failed to be moved by this singular act of bravery, maternal instincts, and disarming courage.

There are other cemeteries in Israel where a vast host of Christians, agnostics, and Eastern believers and others are buried—or who are honored in special tree groves planted in their memory on the stony hills of Jerusalem. Their names are inscribed on tombstones or on garden plaques, often with a brief narrative of their noble audacity.

The Nazis routinely offered a bounty for those who turned in Jews who were hiding. The bounty consisted of a quart of liquor, four pounds of sugar, a carton of cigarettes, or, at times, small cash payments. For many civilians, these commodities were unobtainable through normal channels, and so they were provided with a powerful enticement to cooperate with the *Gestapo*—the bestial central agency whose mission was to find Jews and kill them. Any person or family righteously hiding or rescuing Jews were exterminated outright.

It seems as though no incentive, other than blind human compassion and utter decency, compelled this daring Indian woman to stare down hate and save a baby. The Talmud states: "If you save a single life, you save the whole world."

This is one of oldest Jewish credos ever, and for this we plant trees in the Holy Land.

Holiday memo to preachers: It's God house, not your 'edifice complex'

December 4, 2008

You know, most of us rabbis, ministers, priests, and other clergy came into this line of work with our eyes open and our hearts pure. We're hardly perfect, but we arrived clear-eyed, idealistic, and not jaded. Even though so much of our work is done *outside* the building, in hospitals, cemeteries, community halls, and in family homes, we do think that the vision of a "house of God" can be very redemptive.

I no longer work full-time as a pulpit rabbi, devoting most of my time to my agency work, writing, lecturing, and public seminars that invariably involve interfaith relations. But I shall always be a son of the synagogue and derive deep and immense joy from serving weekly as rabbi of an endearing congregation of 700 elders here in Southern California.

You can't dabble in the spirit all about town without knowing your home address in Scripture. In my case, it's called the Torah and its family narratives, its cry for freedom over slavery, its legislation in favor of property rights, education, and human dignity were studied by me in a synagogue long before I had the gumption to start preaching about it "out there."

"Let them build Me a sanctuary, that I may dwell among them." So it is written in the Book of Exodus. Somewhere, in between the committee meetings, the closed sessions, the personnel discussions, the membership deliberations, and the budget debates—all necessary and commendable—somewhere in there a man or woman "of the cloth" is just supposed to help somebody find God.

Here's something for those clergy who sometimes succumb to an "edifice complex." The place of worship will always be bigger than the preacher or anybody else for that matter. I believe in institutions—synagogues and churches are the coordinates of survival because they grow people with spirit. They harvest our culture, even as they are local, personal, and directly involved in what folks think and feel and fear. They nurture love and they inspire good moral outrage. The church or synagogue is the parent of the YMCA, the JCC, the National Charity League and so on—because it is in the sanctuary that one learns the letters and thereby goes out to complete the alphabet of his or her spiritual commitment.

Though I do other things now, I think my weekly congregation sustains my laughter and sensitivity. Being with them has already reminded me of my roots in this work. It's hard not to be affected by the touch of so many hands, the press of countless huge hugs, the texture of tenderness, the breakthrough moments of study, the whispers of painful secrets shared in clinical privacy, the bitter tears of separation in the cemetery, the joyous tears of bride and groom, the satisfied weeping of parents blessing their children at Torah ceremonies—the salty waters of human life that define, say, a rabbi and a congregation much more than even the finest, consultant-tuned "mission statement."

In this mercantile season that sucks the life out of festivals, it's good to remember what you learned with a prayer book in your hands.

Hanukkah is the clinging narrative of a Jewish land

December 5, 2008

The coming small festival of Hanukkah, made larger only by its calendar proximity to Christmas, is a paradigm of the Jewish spiritual and historical lock on the land of Israel. If the Jewish Maccabees had not managed to expel the religion-killing Greek-Syrians from Judea in 165 BCE, there would have been no more Judaism—a century and a half before Christ. Therefore, no Hanukkah, no Christmas. As ever, the collateral was, has been, and will remain the Jewish connection to the land.

I was born in Israel just a few years after its inception in 1948. My father and mother were there, however, as the British withdrew on May 14 of that year, lowering the Union Jack over the port of Haifa, and raising the stakes considerably for the 600,000 Jews in mandatory Palestine now left to confront a host of Arab nations planning to invade and destroy the nascent Jewish state.

I remember living in that idyllic place as a child. It was long before suicide bombings, murderous plots laid out by dictators who trade oil for blood, and before dreadful skyjackings in Europe and America that somehow had something to do with the sweet osprey birds that flew about the desert of our little homeland.

Many of my classmates in the dusty village of Kfar-Saba were the children of Holocaust survivors who had been rescued by Haganah soldiers like my own father, smuggled into Palestine from Cyprus and other places in the wake of the Nazi insanity. The names in my fourth grade classroom hailed from Russia, Brazil, South Africa, Germany, Poland and Yemen. We all planted onions and sunflowers in the reddish earth around the schoolyard and we sang songs in the free language of Hebrew.

There was a time when you could easily recite the meaning of Israel's birth, and it's worth remembering now. Israel only came into being because Europe had slaughtered the Jews and then because the United Nations had a stunning vote in its Security Council: By a tally of 33 to 13, the UN partitioned Palestine into two states, one Jewish and one Arab. The

Jewish Agency, still heaving from the genocide and desperate to create a sanctuary for the exiles, agreed. The independent Arab nations, manifold times larger than Israel, declared their intention to finish what the Nazis had started. *These are the facts*; even as the ensuing Arab invasion of the Jewish territories served to displace the parallel victims of this blunder—the Palestinian people.

Whether or not the leaders of the Palestinian people still want that separate state or not, or even if they indeed covet the full region and would still plan to consume the sovereign state of Israel, the Palestinian people themselves still need to feel they belong somewhere—just as we Jewish children of the remnant felt we belonged somewhere back in the days following Israel's birth.

But before either one of us, Arab or Jew, can plan the future, we must learn the past. We were both always there in that land, even as the wind brought the Romans, the Crusaders, the Ottomans, the British, and so many others into the land to help set us against each other. My childhood memories include the thick citrus smell of orange groves that lay between Kfar-Saba and the minarets of the neighboring Arab village of Qalqilya. We actually lived in peace; there was no fear in the air—until the plotting Egyptians and Syrians decided to exterminate the Jewish state in 1967 and suddenly every orange tree, every brook of water, every synagogue and every mosque would become a flashpoint.

Israel's birth in 1948, like Hanukkah in 165 BCE, was a heroic and healing response to the politics of murder. In the name of Moses, Jesus, and Mohammed, can't we all have a real Christmas?

Ruby Compton lost her love and her heart on Pearl Harbor Day

December 7, 2008

At Cincinnati's Woodward High School in the later 1960s, some of my buddies and I made fun of Miss Ruby Compton, the redoubtable civics teacher, because she was gangly and outspoken about being a single woman and a professional.

"Miss Compton" was an accomplished and skilled educator but her perpetual personal social status combined with her older age aroused shameful speculations on our part. Years later, I learned from another former teacher at the school that Ruby Compton never married because her fiancé, the love and hero of her life, perished at Pearl Harbor on December 7, 1941, and she decided to turn her empty heart toward the edification of city students. I have never stopped regretting our sophomoric behavior.

I've wondered if any of my scattered buddies (the ones who didn't die in Vietnam) ever discovered this and if they might feel the same little disgrace. We've all gone separate ways and are likely only linked by threads of memory and fading year books. I think of Ruby Compton, departed along with many blessed teachers, every December 7th, which itself is now linked with September 11th as markers of our national vulnerability, our gritty resilience, and our orphans and widows and widowers.

The teacher, now a longtime friend who told me Ruby's secret is Bonnie Kind, now 61. Bonnie, a generation younger than Miss Compton, ironically taught social studies and history—including the seismic narrative of the Japanese attack on December 7, 1941. Bonnie is wistful and she wants to put the best face on her memories of teaching in that tense urban high school during the 1960s.

In truth, she had thrived in her few years at Woodward, made innovations in curricula and after-school programs such as the Council on World Affairs, and valued the mentoring she received from Miss Ruby Compton. The woman we puberty boys derided as awkward and out-of-touch was actually a paradigm hero and survivor—in the most searing personal way—of a Day of Infamy that we did not grasp, perhaps, until our own September 11, 2001.

At some time during those momentous days of the '60s, when people actually still grieved for the drowned and burnt soldiers and sailors of Honululu, Dr. Martin Luther King, Jr. declared:

"All men are interdependent...We are everlasting debtors to known and unknown men and women. When we arise in the morning, we go into the bathroom where we reach for a sponge which is provided for us by a Pacific islander. We reach for soap that is created for us by a European. Then at the table we drink coffee which is provided for us by a South American, or tea by a Chinese, or cocoa by a West African. Before we leave for our jobs we are already beholden to more than half of the world."

Now that the world is 'one,' we seem further apart than ever. God bless you, Miss Compton.

'It's not natural for me to be burying my child'

December 8, 2008

When a father loses a child, he loses part of his immortality. When a mother loses a child, she loses something that grew in her womb. Yesterday, both Murray and Jean M. suffered egregiously as they laid their adult daughter Diane to rest in a California cemetery. Not even the forgiving December sunshine could break up the darkness that set in on the hillside where we spoke prayers, leaning against one another along the unwelcome slope.

It was not the first time that I've heard a mother or father cry out with the desperate anger of this worst nightmare of human life. Sadly, as a rabbi, I have buried babies, teenagers, and adult children of all ages. They were suicides, victims of abuse, drugs, drowning, car accidents, and even murder. Of course some succumbed to cancer, HIV, congenital heart defects, and other ailments that are as much of part of life as the sunlight on a California hillside.

Diane, a daughter, wife, mother, grandmother, and sister, was born in 1953 and lived a rich and meaningful life, delighting and challenging her family and friends with wit, insight, and strong opinions. The truth is she was not a well-known individual, nor an inventor, and hardly a celebrity. Her brief life will not go down in documented history and her death from pancreatic cancer is more a matter of record than journalistic sensation. And in all this was the sad beauty of this teary gathering of family—a decidedly post-denominational circle of New York ethnics, Utah free spirits, tie-wearing, denim-garbed, coiffed, long-haired, tightly-woven, and free-spirited folks of all classes.

Mortality is the common denominator of the human condition and love leavens cultural issues. Diane was no hero on the earth but she will be well received in heaven. It's one thing to teach people about tenderness by the way you live. It's something else altogether when you teach people about humanity by the way you die.

I reached out to Dan, her husband, a soft-skinned, bespectacled thin man with a long ponytail and a heart as good as God. "I am so sorry," I told him. "I won't even attempt to put together some formula of words to offer you because this is just so dreadful." Dan found the words for me: "Rabbi, I am the luckiest man in the world. I had her and loved her for 36 years."

When Diane's brother Richard first attempted to speak, he broke down and appeared unable to continue. A former cop now in a suit, thick-chested but powerful, he wanted to explain how much he loved his sister even though they had been (as most siblings are) pretty contentious and, in their mother's spontaneous phrase, "loving adversaries.

An uncle got up and put his arm around Richard, declaring, "Here, we'll cry together." The support was visceral and redeeming. Richard suddenly was able to speak mellifluously and the crowd sighed continually in laughter and tears. From then on, every family member who spoke was followed up by someone else who just stood by and offered an arm, a shoulder, a tissue, a good word.

Who could look upon this completely honest human endeavor and not know there is a God?

And yet: One is left above all with the ringing cry in his ears from a *mother*—God's partner in human creation: "It's not natural for me to burying my child."

Let every minister of war consider the mother's cry and no longer add to the inexplicable work that angels must do when parents come into a cemetery.

This Jewish survivor smiled again—in a Catholic church

Undated

Elie Wiesel, the poet laureate of the Holocaust, is perhaps the best known survivor of the genocide. As a young man from the Carpathian Mountains, he lost his family, his friends, and for a time, his soul. In many books, including *Night*, no one has described the Nazi insanity with more searing and unforgiving candor than this gentle writer and teacher.

Several years ago, I was privileged to be part of a panel that interviewed Elie Wiesel before an audience in New York City. All evening, as I sat next to him, I observed the deep lines of experience and suffering that are woven into this tragic icon's face. Looking into his eyes is a mystical passage: These are wells of permanent pain that nonetheless convey a certain tortured belief in humankind. Wiesel, who saw babies hung, is soft-spoken, wiry, uncompromising in his demand for human dignity.

When my turn came to ask him a question, I inquired: "Professor Wiesel, after the war ended and you were finally freed from the concentration camps, when was the first time you were able to smile again?"

The Nobel laureate paused momentarily, but then he raised his eyebrows in recognition of a restored memory. "Yes," he said, "I recall the moment."

He then proceeded to recount a long walk he took within a year or so of the close of the war. It was along a rural road in France, where he has often lived since 1945. He explained that, as he made his way, he thought he heard the sound of singing voices. He then realized that he was approaching a country church.

Wiesel, persecuted and tortured by the Germans because he was a Jew, felt drawn to the doorway of the abbey. Inside, he gazed at and heard an exuberant group of children, in luscious robes, singing hymnals together under the busy direction of their choirmaster.

"They were beautiful children," he told us, his eyes watering. "They sang like angels, in Latin. There was a pure and simple joy about them. I did not understand the words of their liturgy but I felt the utter truth of their expression. I felt a truth that transcended their language and their faith. It was then, at that moment, that I felt myself breaking into a smile again for the first time."

Wiesel seemed truly transformed and the hall filled with thunderous applause. As the crowd finally quieted, he added, wistfully, "I truly haven't thought of that since it happened a lifetime ago."

At this holiday season, when religion is too often impaired by indoctrination, consider the testimony of one who survived a wretched childhood in the kingdom of death. What God would not have taken pleasure in the sound made by such Catholic children in the ears of a sorrowing Jew in that countryside that had just been the landscape of hell?

Saw the '68 Impala go by and thought of my Dad

December 11, 2008

He was a classic immigrant; eager to learn the language and the citizenship codes. He earned his American papers legitimately and with a glowing pride, expecting no favors, passes, or benefits until he earned them with civil integrity. He memorized the Bill of Rights, took the oath with his right hand up in allegiance and poignancy, and then bought a flag pole for our sparkling new Old Glory on the way home.

He stocked up on Coca-Cola, set up the barbecue grill in the little patch of a backyard that was for him the equivalent of a homestead, and then paid cash for the ultimate prize: a sky-blue Chevrolet Impala with automatic transmission, push-button locks, and, God in heaven, air conditioning! GM was the iconic tower brand of the USA, baseball was still a game, presidents were appropriately remote and thereby gigantic, gasoline was divided into regular and Ethyl and served by actual men who talked to you and checked your oil and we didn't even know that it had anything to do with Arab cartels or even somebody else's religion.

My father drove his chromatic Chevy to work at General Electric, where he helped design the heat shield for the Gemini space ships that carried two astronauts at a time in a space race that we were winning over the Soviet Union. There were absolutes in the world (though, in fairness, many troubling things that remained obscured by our strong belief in the strength and nobility of our government), but one thing that remained absolute was the fact that the rest of the world respected and adored us and also wanted our Chevys and the Coca-Colas.

So, the other day, as I cruised along in my German-made car, and a proud, stubborn, freshly painted 1968 Chevrolet Impala passed me by, its six rear lights twinkling in nostalgic dismissal, I remembered my Dad and the simpler times. The Chevy was neither sleek nor aerodynamic but it didn't have to be. It was, like my Dad's vehicle a long time ago, a little arrogant, bottom-heavy, and solid as the faith we had in nation, public schools, postal delivery, the ever-loving greenback, and Dads themselves.

Detroit had a normal good year in '68, and even a good ball club, and incidentally, Opening Day was played in the USA and not in Japan or some other place that had more clout than Ohio or Illinois and even more dollars. My father's bedrock belief in his Chevy automobile was as strong as his differences of opinion with our nation's polices in Indochina and towards our black minority that was finally being heard in the trumpet sound of Martin Luther King, Jr. and a million other human rights soldiers who believed enough in our institutions to even bleed for them.

But it really wasn't all that much about the trouble in the world back then that I recalled when I saw the noble '68 "heavy Chevy" that drifted by and then disappeared. I just remembered what my Dad's face looked like when we pulled up at the state park picnic bench in the Impala, opened the truck, retrieved the burgers, turned on the ball game real loud on the Delco radio, and he thought that the USA was heaven.

You lost your job; I've been where you are

December 14, 2008

In the wake of so many professional layoffs, at all levels, I remember when it happened to me: In 2000, I was discharged from a venerable institution that I had served for nearly fifteen years. Granted, it's always complicated when a clergyperson departs a congregation; there are delicate and profound relationships that linger in the mind or dwell in the heart. There is a myriad of unfinished situations. The privilege of leading a house of God has a lot to do with the window into human lives that you are granted. What is ultimately a business decision by an employer is surely layered emotionally when the daily work had everything to do with the business of human life.

These days, I certainly sit with men and women who have also found themselves, for whatever reason, in between jobs. Now I truly discern what they are feeling, even as I have come to understand how common this predicament is in today's cruel economy. Corporate heads, teachers, journalists, artists, mechanics, entrepreneurs—so many different kinds of folks are out there, struggling with some of the same doubts and fears that I've had and that changed my smug view of life forever.

People would call up and ask, what do you do all day? You certainly do a lot of thinking. It's amazing how many things come to the mind when you suddenly find yourself with time to reflect. The search through the soul is, at once, intimidating and revealing. What did the years mean? Where did I succeed, and where did I fail? When you're in the midst of a job, you rarely ask yourself the kinds of questions that define yourself because you're too busy reacting, creating, or submitting to the tyranny of the calendar and the demands of the position itself. It's too much about what you are, not who you are.

An irony: You learn a lot about the dynamics of the work experience once you separate from it. A job and a person can be at war with each other, or they can complement one another, or, more likely, they arrive at some kind of tempered standoff. In the midst of the job, you assume that it is what you are supposed to do. You don't really have the time nor is our professional culture very well suited to help you think about what you are supposed to be. I recognize this now, and relate very deeply with every single person in any kind of calling who has found himself or herself remembering a job rather than doing it.

I believe that this period of both anguish and insight deepened my understanding of human life.

My then-teenage daughters found themselves in the awkward situation of wondering how to behave around their suddenly present father. The daughter who was away at college telephoned a lot, chattering about her schedule, her budget, her plans. She was abnormally concerned about everything that is normal. She listened for my spirit and she clung to my words—undoubtedly groping for reassurance that I was neither scared nor downtrodden. I did my best to reassure her.

My younger daughter, who was still in town for high school, could not dispense with this unfamiliar situation via a telephone conversation or an email transmission. We had breakfast together, and I was usually still at home when she went off to school—a new circumstance. Since mine was a rather public position, her classmates alternated between comforting her and avoiding her.

Someone once said that when one door closes, another one opens. In my case, many doorways have opened. How often do professional middle-aged men truly contemplate the significance of their marriages in long, uninterrupted doses of introspection? How many things do we take for granted in the press of the daily workload? Humbling and worthwhile are the moments of suddenly enforced realization about your ultimate sources of strength and your unqualified spaces for retreat and renewal.

Who actually loves you and whom do you truly love? You sometimes have to get off the train and walk by yourself near the tracks to figure this out. It's lonely and frightening along the path, but it is redeeming. What friends are unconditional, eschewing judgment in favor of compassion and understanding—even when their own lives remain complicated and unresolved? It sometimes take just such a crucible to discover which lives are verily intertwined with your own and who never looked at you as the professional as much as the person.

There is uncertainty in all of this, and this is very much the testing of one's patience and discipline and faith. Some days are better than others. So many of us are driven—by the Web, cellular phones, electronic calendars.

We take a great deal for granted, including the presumption of power and entitlement. In so many jobs, we acquire much, but we gain little—including gratitude for the lives that inform our own.

I feel a strengthening of my spirit—even on days when my spirit is stooped and weakened. I feel that whatever I do, I will be enriched by a professional separation that, slowly, agonizingly, granted me the knowledge and humility that comes with rediscovering the unyielding power of human love and the enlightening need to listen to others. But what I feel the most is that there is a lot of anonymous suffering out there.

'Somehow, the prayers just fall out of your heart'

December 15, 2008

She visited the regal chapel at the University of Notre Dame, South Bend, Indiana recently. As with everything else, she took it in with full soul and fond disposition. Strong-limbed yet tender-hearted, she sought the relief of a sanctuary in the midst of her usual tyranny of business meetings and corporate competition. She's an executive out there, but I know her in her natural manifestation: my beloved friend, my wife, muse, and partner.

Looking for respite in the cold sojourn, she found her way to the Basilica of the Sacred Heart, with origins in the 17th century and based upon the Church of the Gesù in Rome, the mother church of the Society of Jesus designed by Giacomo Barozzi da Vignola in 1568. Audrey, born a Catholic, but who describes her self-driven, teenage journey to Judaism as "a return to my spiritual roots," does not feel that God is exclusive to any space. She shares with me the sense that Judaism's hallmark is the fact that it *parented* Christianity –in this concept is the foundation of our independent, interfaith, and nonjudgmental pastoral agency, Reconciliation: The Synagogue Without Walls, which we founded together in 2004.

The four children that we share in this second marriage, ranging in age from 28 to 13, from theater artist to video wizard, with a literary scholar and a teenage environmentalist in between, know that we regard faith as a deeply personal matter that inspires acts of social justice.

Our family gatherings for birthdays and holidays, from Passover to Christmas, are the constant realizations (not without normal frictions and resentments) of the best face of religiosity. We are, thank God, a completely integrated cross-bred family of Jews, Christians, agnostics, Colombians, Canadians, New Yorkers, Buckeyes, and, oh yes, my Israeli mother. It's a cultural pastiche of hummus and empanadas and the liturgy is love.

So Audrey traveled to the plains of Indiana to discuss variable annuities but she took a brisk walk on the campus of one of the most esteemed Christian colleges on the continent. Taking time to reflect in the Basilica, she then wrote me these words: "Entering a house of prayer has a way of making you reflect on what's really important in your life and somehow the prayers just fall out of your heart."

If only all the righteous rectors, cardinals, rabbis, imams, had gotten this memo.

The Nativity Story is lifted out of the pages of Genesis

December 16, 2008

Pretty much the same story appeared and was told a long time before.

Religious traditions borrow heavily from one another; they are really a series of sacred tales woven, and eventually canonized, in one way or another. In its simplicity and luminosity, the Nativity is unrivaled—it certainly has lifted the souls of millions of people for thousands of years.

Just as the Creation story has roots in earlier Babylonian narratives, it's hard not to blueprint the birth chronicle of Jesus in a much earlier drama found in the eighteenth chapter of Genesis—very early in the Hebrew Scripture. The elderly Abraham was sitting in the tent door on an extremely hot day and "the Lord appeared unto him by the trees of Mamre." Sarah, his wife was inside the tent; they had been married for a long time, through many passages, but had never borne a child together. In fact, as the Torah makes exceedingly clear, Sarah could no longer conceive.

The old Scripture relates that Abraham "lifted up his eyes and looked, and, lo, three men stood over against him." *Three* men: We already know that these three are a composite of God and the fact that there are *three* cannot be lost upon those who recall the "three wise men" of the New Testament. Although there are other ramifications in this episode, the key element is that the three men, actually three angels, notify Abraham that he and Sarah will finally have a son.

In a bittersweet moment that follows, Sarah "laughs" at the idea: "After I am waxed old shall I have pleasure; my lord being old also?" She knows better—the women in Scripture usually do. But she does give birth to Isaac even as the Torah does not resolve the fact that she is postmenopausal.

Just four chapters later, Abraham is "tested" by God. This is perhaps the most wrenching episode that Jewish readers of Scripture discuss; it is read and examined in many synagogues at Rosh Hashanah. God demands of the elderly Abraham: "Take now thy son, thine only son, whom thou lovest…and sacrifice him upon one of the mountains which I tell thee of."

Of course, the drama concludes when Abraham, about to actually put a knife through Isaac and make a burnt offering of him, is stayed by an angel of God: "For now I know that thou art a God-fearing man, seeing thou has not withheld thy son, thine only son, from Me.

There is a quick exchange of the boy for a *lamb*, of all things. Good stories live and are recast because people with imagination and faith want to help somebody else feel hope. The moral of this one, from the Jewish point of view, is that people do not sacrifice their own children to please a God; would that today's radicalized "theologians" finally get that as they carry on their "holy wars."

Our first annual 'Restless Spirits' awards
December 18, 2008

The Annual SLE (Spiritual Life Examiner) Restless Spirits Awards are not judg-ment-driven. That is to say, being a 'Restless Spirit' is not necessarily a bad thing or a good thing. But it's definitely a thing to notice. The five finalists stood out be-cause, whatever their motivations or principles or even spiritual tribulations, they were exemplary and had the guts to stand in the public glare. We are unable to re-sist a prediction for each of our awardees. Your comments are welcome; perhaps we can settle on the big prize before New Year's!

GOV. SARAH PALIN: Courageous and outspoken, never mind syntax, in spite of churning ambitions, and a stubborn eye tic. <u>Prediction</u>: Will be tapped as Ambassador to Russia.

PRESIDENT BILL CLINTON: Unable to distinguish between an actual conviction (uh, spiritual, not legal) and an annoying reporter. Either set him off on sermonic tsunamis—give the man credit for struggling publicly with a chronic internal filibuster. <u>Prediction</u>: You guessed it; it will have to be explained by the Department of State, even if it happened in Zimbabwe.

OPRAH WINFREY: Continues to bare soul and body, especially the latter, in the category of metabolic angst. Really diverting as banks and corpora-tions fail. <u>Prediction</u>: Will try to put a little meat on Obama's bones, but to no avail.

ANGELINA JOLIE: Mother of any given day and continues to eradicate world hunger and child depravation, one limo and 47 nannies per child. <u>Prediction</u>: Will continue not to burden Academy of Motion Picture Arts and Sciences selection committee but will beat up many more men.

O.J. SIMPSON: Poignantly begged for understanding in Las Vegas court-room; "I just wanted my stuff back." On par with many teary "Forgive me my sins" preachments of some fallen televangelists. <u>Prediction</u>: Will find the real killer in prison laundry room.

Oy vey, what's the deal with the 'Jesus eyes'?

December 19, 2008

Somebody else noticed it before me. My friend, a salt of the earth in his eighties who fought the Germans at Normandy and then made it all the way to Berlin, is not easily persuaded by theological whimsies and he is hardly star struck. But watching the television promotional ad for the Barack Obama *"Victory Plate"* recently (one of scores of bald-faced, disingenuous, and manipulative ads that exploit Barack Obama's ascent to the presidency), he could not help but notice the two pools of divinity in the senator's visage.

"My God, the fellow has 'Jesus eyes,'" my friend told me over the telephone. Watching the same presentation myself, in between the Barack Minted Coins and the Michelle Inaugural Fashion Tapestry, I saw it for myself. Transcending Kenyan roots and Hawaiian lineage, freed even of the bonds *terra Chicago*, Barack Obama stares out from his Victory Plate with the eyes of heaven. May the One deliver the nourishment of such a saucer.

Senator Barack Obama, electoral mortal, is nonetheless the winner of this year's "Most Likely to Have Jesus Eyes" award.

Tonight, a child will defeat all the darkness
December 21, 2008

Why do we believe, after all these centuries of bestial treatment by so many of the strong of so many of the weak, after countless wars in which men ordered the slaughter of children in the name of their gods, after Munich and now Mumbai, that Hanukkah's little songs are worth singing, that its little candles are worth lighting?

Why do we so heartily delight in the calendar coincidence of Christian children lighting candles this week as well, even as the arrival of Hanukkah tonight sheds further light on the culminating Advent? Why do we rejoice particularly this year, when the first of the eight lights of Hanukkah will break through the December 21 solstice itself, sending a beam into the darkest night of the entire year?

Why did the rabbinic tradition try very hard to actually downgrade the military aspect of the original Hanukkah rebellion in 165 BCE against the Greek Syrians—in favor of a spiritual celebration that embraces miracles, parents blessing their children, and putting a candelabrum in the nighttime window?

We feel this way, about a little festival that sheds star shine on all the others, of all the faiths, because the Jewish people have always defeated brutality with the power of ideas.

We believe that the best interpretation of the nasty little war that took place in Judea back then, during which Jewish volunteers threw out the Hellenistic-spouting despots who denied us the right to practice our faith, who defiled our temples with pig statuettes, who banned our liturgies from the land we had inherited biblically, who made the speaking of Hebrew a capital crime—all this we vowed to remember not in military terms but in small games, miracle-loving canticles, the sharing of potato pancakes, and the spinning of dreidels. We eschewed the necessary blood of Hanukkah in favor of the veneration of holy oil. We removed the tyrants from Israel and made little children the royalty of the world.

That's what Hanukkah really is, and that is what happens tonight when a child lights one candle. What that child feels in his or her heart, that complete innocence and pure trust, and the attendant beam of light shattering the solstice—is there any power truly greater than that?

Happy Hanukkah to every child and every grown-up who ever gave up hope!

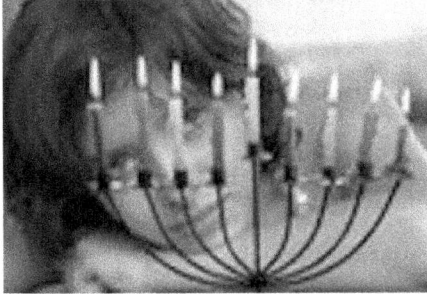

For Christmas, we'd like Jerusalem, no returns necessary

December 22, 2008

Given that this is a season of the "wish list," let me offer, on behalf of my people, that we'd like the gift of Jerusalem. This would be easy enough to offer on the part of the rest of the world—the city was founded and developed by Jewish kings and priests three thousand years ago, it has never served as the capital of anything but two Jewish commonwealths ever since, and it has functioned as a unified city (for the past 41 years) only in Jewish hands.

The administration of the whole city of Jerusalem by Israel was instigated by the Jordanian shelling of the western "Israeli side" in June, 1967—as Israel was responding to yet another massive Egyptian/Syrian build-up and openly published threats on the part of the Arab world to exterminate the Jewish state. (Americans are now well-acquainted with the standing Islamic intention to wipe out the American way of life and faith).

The Jordanians had forcefully occupied the eastern section of the venerated city since 1949—for those who like to bandy the term "occupation" in association with the state of Israel. The good people who lived there were Jordanian citizens, and placed Jordanian license plates on their cars. I saw this myself when I visited the reunified city just weeks after the Six Day War in 1967. I've seen a city grow dramatically in infrastructure, skyline, cultural institutions, tourism, and prestige during my many visits since. Israel has to address some significant disparities in housing, schools, and social services that plague some Arab neighborhoods, just as New York has to rebuild its ghettos, Amsterdam has to clean up its rampant drug addiction, Beijing has to make its air breathable, and Teheran has to let women walk about the city in comfortable clothing and without male chaperones.

In the category of spirituality, Israel, since 1967, has maintained access to the holy sites of all faiths in Jerusalem, while dealing with Islamic suicide bombings, the looming Iranian nuclear threat, the sudden Palestinian claim to Jerusalem as its capital (even though Jerusalem is not mentioned in the Koran and is third in sanctity for Muslims after Mecca and Medina) and the incongruous (oil-drenched) failure of other democratic nations to recognize Jerusalem as the federal capital of the only democracy in the region. This, in spite of the fact that Israel turned over control of the Temple Mount to the *Wakf*—the Moslem Religious Trust. This, in spite of the fact that during the Jordanian occupation from 1949 to 1967, the Jewish Quarter was ransacked, Jewish cemeteries violated, and Arab snipers routinely shot at Jewish residents on the "other side."

But there is no "side" to this. Jesus changed the world from Jewish Jerusalem. With some 500 references to the city in the Hebrew Scripture, dating as far back as Abraham, no logical conclusion exists other than that Jerusalem is a Jewish city and has been for far longer than Washington, DC has been the capital of the United States. This is as certain as the fact that on Christmas morning, the electricity will flow and the plumbing will work in a special city that needs management as much as it inspires prayer.

Postscript: Top 5 spiritual train wrecks of 2008 Palin comparison
December 23, 2008

Gov. Rod Blagojevich may or may not answer to state and federal authorities for his brazen auctioning of President-elect Barack Obama's vacated Senate seat. But he's likely to answer to the court of heaven for his incongruous use of a *children's hospital* as bait in one of his currency schemes. The good governor apparently threatened to rescind $8 million in Illinois funds for a children's medical facility because someone neglected to offer up a campaign contribution.
Recommendation: Rod serves as a diaper-changer in same hospital.

Bernard Madoff's heinous financial crimes hurt the philanthropic causes of his own community in particular and with stunning injury. In his self-absorbed fog, he became the O.J. Simpson of hedge funds.
Recommendation: Bernie bakes and serves Hanukkah cookies to the homeless and hungry up and down Los Angeles' Sepulveda Boulevard.

Madonna is in great physical condition (caught her callisthenic performance in San Diego the night Obama won) but she droops in the category of the spirit. She pummeled her publicist for releasing the settlement figures related to her divorce (yes, divorce is actually the end of a marriage). The early release of the numbers was meant to imply her generosity (this is too funny) but it backfired in the media and so the lady let her PR person take the fall.
Recommendation: Madonna takes night classes about the real Madonna.

Sen. Hillary Clinton broke down and cried on the eve of the New Hampshire primary. In all fairness, the late Sen. Edmund Muskie wept during a snowy primary in 1972 and thereby lost his momentum towards the Democratic presidential nomination. Clinton's spiritual meltdown, a product of fatigue and entitlement, propelled her to a surprise victory.
Recommendation: Secretary of State Clinton weeps in Gaza, creating shame and conciliation and a peace agreement.

Gov. Eliot Spitzer was disgraced out of office in Albany after revelations of his vivid involvement in a luxury prostitution ring. This, after the man propelled himself (excuse the expression) into office as a tough reformer who would clean up all the corruption in New York.
<u>Recommendation</u>: Still thinking.

THIS JUST IN : **Gov. Sarah Palin** today declared that she would have done better in the campaign had she been able to "call the shots" more and grant more interviews. This now leads all entries as a 2008 spiritual train wreck. Here is the evidence, verbatim, spoken by the Republican vice-presidential nominee: (Source: The *New York Times*)

> *My concern has been the atrocities there in Darfur and the relevance to me with that issue as we spoke about Africa and some of the countries there that were kind of the people succumbing to the dictators and the corruption of some collapsed governments on the continent, the relevance was Alaska's investment in Darfur with some of our permanent fund dollars.*

Let us close this contest now with a prayer for the English language.

Tonight, two lights will be better than one
December 24, 2008

A benevolent calendar coincidence, occurring every few years, brings us on Dec. 24 to the shared lighting of solstice calendars by both Christians and Jews. The solar and lunar calendar cycles have intertwined, and so this Christmas eve will share the fourth night of Hanukkah, 5769. The circumstances should work to everyone's advantage on Earth and must be pleasing to the heavens.

Because the December holiday season, formally entwined this year, is too often undermined by commercial anxiety and social stresses, we might find serenity in the gentle purposes undertaken today in the name of Scripture. Didn't Judah and his Maccabees fight for the very right that Christians enjoy to feel the birth of a messianic dream? Didn't Jesus preach to the very benevolence that Christians must feel as they look out their windows and see their neighbor's candelabra glowing?

Neither holiday is fully realized without the acknowledgment of the other.

Although they derive from different stories, their outcomes are really the same: Give children some hope, shared values among all the valuables exchanged, and the Torah is revealed while the Gospel is made true. God looks down and sees that little ones are making light.

Jews should light our fourth candle tonight in gratitude for the peace and security that we enjoy at this special solstice. The 20th century was uncommonly harsh for us, and we too often could not collect enough wax for even one Hanukkah candle. The United States at the close of 2008, war-fatigued and economically stricken, nonetheless shared in an historic election in terms of numbers and outcome.

We Jews should note: In the past generation, more Christians have done more soul-searching about who Jesus the Jew actually was than in many centuries. Christian interest in the Jewish calendar and in the welfare of the state of Israel is unprecedented.

Christians should look upon their wreaths not only as winter décor, but as the true crown of Christ. In doing this, they will learn more about the meaning and history of Hanukkah: It was, after all, the original rebellion against religious tyranny, occurring in 168 B.C.E. It paved the way for the notion of theological freedom—from the Maccabees to Paul to Mohammed to the founding parents of U.S. democracy.

The fact that December's days are particularly short gives this year's shared lights added luminance. We Jews think of the power of ideas that overcame the brutality back then at the original Hanukkah, and our children get special insight into the yearning for freedom that still grips the globe, from Zimbabwe to Iraq to China.

Christians, hopefully inspired by the incandescence of the messianic idea and innocence of a baby-child who changed the world, should think of what Christmas means to the soul, and not to the budget. Hanukkah has also become a hostage to the issue of credit, when all the Maccabees wanted credit for what was the very right Jesus had—185 years later—to save a light from going out.

Let both houses remember that what the Maccabees died for and what Jesus was born for was to build a world safe enough for a child to see through the darkness. The day is short, but together, we make hope long.

The 5 things every Jew does on Christmas

December 25, 2008

Sincere and dearest holiday wishes to our friends in the Christian community celebrating the birth of hope on this holiest and happiest day of the year! We share in the spirit of this day; we commemorate the festival by proxy, even as this is an official American public holiday.

Not infrequently am I asked by well-meaning neighbors, "What do Jewish people do on Christmas?" Here, in fun and cheer, are my definitive five answers:

* **Have brunch** with family members, calling it 'the December 25 holiday meal.' *Note: No alcohol is consumed because we invariably will attend the Christmas Open House of our Nice Gentile Neighbors in the late afternoon. This also alleviates the discussion of dinner (highly examined at lunch), although only for now.*

* **Debate** which drug store is actually open even though it is Christmas. *We will invariably "need something," most likely hydrocortisone lotion or the shampoo with zinc. We will, in the tradition of social justice, feel bad for the employees working there on Christmas but be so thrilled it's open.*

* **Wonder** how much money Barbra Streisand has made on all those Christmas albums. *Neil Young, too, and what's the guy who made "The Jazz Singer?"*

* **Marvel** at the potency of that mixture in the big punch bowl at the Christmas Open House. *They're really not eating anything either so we should save it maybe for dinner out after all. What is egg nog, really?*

* **Eat dinner** at the Chinese place. *This is like Torah. We really have nothing in common with these nice people who work here and we don't know what holiday they are not celebrating but they're the only ones open. Oy, pass the General Tso's.*

Before the receding and breathless year of 2008 finally ended, a fierce war broke out in the Gaza Strip, and the world watched, prayed, and also criticized. But first, a respite, almost as vivid as it was in 1968, recalling the Apollo 8 moon mission and the Christmas message of hope broadcast back to Earth by the astronauts.

Forty years ago, they read the Bible to us from the moon

December 26, 2008

A man in a space suit read the first ten verses of Scripture to us as he hurtled through space.

Apollo 8, the redemptive moon mission of December 1968, was the first manned voyage to return to earth from another celestial body. Astronauts Frank Borman, James Lovell, and William Anders, who were navigating the capsule back home 40 years ago this week, were the first human beings to see the dark side of the moon with their own eyes.

They were also the first three people to send a Christmas message back to the entire planet Earth while orbiting the moon. Their courage, discipline, and timing were unparalleled and there could have no more healing conclusion to the paroxysmal year of 1968. The fact is that America *seemed* like the dark side of the moon in 1968.

Dr. Martin Luther King, Jr., 39, was assassinated on April 4 while standing on his hotel balcony in Memphis. Eight weeks later, Sen. Robert F. Kennedy, 42, was gunned down in the kitchen of the Ambassador Hotel in Los Angeles. The nation convulsed under these twin assassinations, the rampant urban riots that cascaded in their wake, and a sense of hopelessness about the spiraling Vietnam War, the electoral system itself (bloody rioting almost shut down the Democratic National Convention in Chicago), and a desperately close presidential race that gave us the spectral Richard Nixon. The retiring president, Lyndon Johnson, who had succeeded the murdered President John F. Kennedy in 1963, was basically hounded from office.

We literally looked heavenward as the December holidays approached and the three heroes were launched into space by the thrust of a 36-story Saturn rocket. Our nation was weary, forlorn, uncertain, and in need of heavenly hope. TIME Magazine recalled what happened in a retrospective:

That evening, as families finished their Christmas Eve dinners, the astronauts pointed their camera out the window and beamed home a grainy, gray view of the alien world they were circling. Everywhere on the planet, viewers tuned in, making up what was then the largest TV audience in history. Borman, Lovell and Anders had been instructed to do whatever they felt was appropriate to mark the moment. A friend of Borman's had suggested they read from the book of Genesis, and so its first 10 verses had been typed up on a piece of fireproof paper before the crew left Earth. They took turns reading aloud.

When they finished, Borman, as the skipper, concluded the broadcast: "And from the crew of Apollo 8," he said, "we close with good night, good luck, a merry Christmas, and God bless all of you, all of you on the good Earth."

"In the beginning, God created the heaven and the earth."

It keeps being recreated.

From the point of spirit, Israel's Gaza operation is overdue

December 28, 2008

Israel's agonizing incursion into the Gaza region, reminiscent of ancient Israel's recurring quandary with the inexorable Philistines (of the same area), represents a painful predicament for a democratic government trying to protect its citizens from rocket fire and suicide bombings.

One might have actually hoped that after the residents of Gaza, a strip of misery along the Mediterranean that is historically Egyptian, had chosen the Hamas party in a free election, some civic and cultural restoration would have begun. Hamas is an organization burned onto the official United States list of banned terrorist organizations, along with Al Qaeda and other such Islamic outfits. Hamas proved its mettle by a subsequent bestial takeover of the entire Gaza government that featured mass killings of Fatah (its Palestinian opponent) families and the throwing of men and women from rooftops.

Hamas has since seized the opportunity over the past couple of years not to rebuild schools, hospitals, and infrastructure, but to launch unending missile attacks into Israeli cities, kidnap Israeli soldiers, and remain a poster child for the international Islamic holy war against Americans. America is still intact, Israel will be criticized for doing whatever a sane nation would do to pacify its borders, and—here is the saddest thing of all—all those innocent children in Gaza who've never really gone to school, enjoyed fresh water, hot meals, and a chance to dream will be further robbed of any prospect of childhood.

If a similar pattern of terror and shock had been festering along the U.S.-Mexican border all these years (and this is not a model frontier), and San Diego, Nogales, AZ, and Laredo, TX were being bombed and bloodied relentlessly, not too many folks would have questioned an American response on behalf of its citizens. But Israel is uniquely quarantined in the international circle of hypocrisy: Its capital, Jerusalem, is constantly being turned over hypothetically to Palestinians, Jordanians, or UN commissions, even as nobody is asking the Canadian parliament in Ottawa to give the Hull section back to a Quebec cut-off, nobody is petitioning that we return Ohio to the Mohicans or Florida to the Seminoles, or that Northern Ireland be restored to the Irish.

Meanwhile, I want my little niece in Ashdod, Israel to stop having to worry about *Ketushya* rockets burning her skin and I'd like my cousin in Tel Aviv to run his hotel and enjoy his family without the specter of an Iranian nuke. But in my heart I'd just as soon like the little kid in Gaza, who lives in mud and ignorance, not to be used one more day as a pawn in some *jihad* fanatic's war against normal civilization.

Part 2: This thing about Jewish and Palestinian children

December 29, 2008

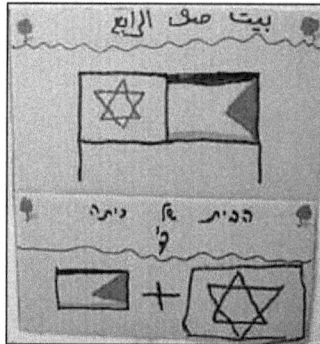

A number of reactions to my piece yesterday about the sad inevitability of Israel's current operation in Gaza (these were received through various mediums) continued the mantra questioning Israel's "right to exist." Ironically, some of these spiritually pejorative incitements come from misguided (I think) Bible-thumping Christians, whose earthly connections to the Holy Land depend upon the State of Israel's unconditional, 60-year defense of all the holy sites that connect people of all faiths to Scripture.

Would some of these folks prefer that the Church of the Holy Sepulcher in Jerusalem be turned over to the kind ministrations of Hamas? Do they yearn to have Bethlehem colonized as an Al Qaeda regional bureau?

When I wrote yesterday about my little niece near Ashdod, Israel, being afraid of Hamas bombs, my family had not received word yet that, in fact, her little village of Gan Yavneh was indeed strafed and she sat sobbing in the family "security room" while my frantic and worried brother called home from his office in Jerusalem. And even though some readers accused me of insensitivity to the myriads of Gaza children suffering through the Israeli air strikes, did they suddenly lose their literacy skills when it came to those sections of my posting that lamented *exactly that*?

You can't love a child in Israel and suddenly forget what a child is all about in Gaza or Lebanon or Iraq. Unless you so despise children that you use them for decades as pawns in your own sickly Islamic machismo plot to get a whole culture mobilized against a Jewish state just because it is a success in the midst of your abyss. Unless you turn your entire scriptural tradition into a blueprint for an insane "holy war" against playgrounds, school houses, supermarkets, and synagogues.

The drawing shown comes from the *Neve Shalom* ('Oasis of Peace') School in Israel—one of several schools, agencies, and camps in Israel that have sprung up over the years to eradicate hatred at the primary level. What's really happening now in Gaza? Kids are being sent to find crazy killers who murder kids and, in the process, other kids are dying and even the ministering angels are wondering whatever happened to Christmas.

The best miracle of 2008 that no one knows about

December 30, 2008

No one will ever really know what goes on in the basement laundry of the children's hospital in question. That's part of what makes "the blessing of the hands" so miraculous—it doesn't involve publicity agents, news anchors, or RSS feeds.

But what I saw will never be forgotten: While visiting the facility, I met an aged but vibrant Episcopalian *madre* performing a decidedly priestly function that likely has helped saved many little lives. Without fuss or fanfare, she routinely enters the windowless room and speaks quietly to the predominantly Mexican workers. They are responsible for cleaning and sterilizing the surgical instruments before the scalpels, scissors, and such are antiseptically delivered to the doctors and nurses above.

These skilled professionals then operate on children with cancer, congenital heart problems, cystic fibrosis, and a myriad of other dreadful conditions that have flanked childhood. It's to the physicians that we anoint the well-deserved credit for so often saving young lives. But the quiet workers down below deliver instruments free of bacteria so the *madre* blesses their hands before they soak, steam, and purify. That's it—no coverage, no drama, no frills. The woman blesses their hands. They look forward to it and when asked, one of them explained to me, "We don't need anybody to know. We just need to have our hands blessed so the knives will be clean and the children will live."

Forget about all the big wonders of 2008, the election of an African-American president, the successful completion of the Beijing Olympiad without terrorism or environmental asphyxiation, the survival somehow of the American economy, the proliferation of HD television, the transformation of Britney Spears back to lean and viable.

When I saw the *madre* bless the hands, I realized again how insignificant I really am, and that was actually the best miracle of all.

January, 2009

A new beginning, a sense of hope, a relief from the despondency that had penetrated the marrow of American life

Our little year-end film festival of faith, doubt, Holocaust, and hope

January 2, 2009

A crop of genuinely artistic, highly motivating, even spiritually bending motion pictures sent great crowds to the theaters during the Christmas-New Year's hiatus. My wife Audrey and I, eschewing holiday travel in favor of relaxation and reflection in and around home with our children and family, made it our business to view a host of the films which arrived, like welcome prize-seeking birds, all at once.

Slumdog Millionaire took our breath away with its Dickensesque fairy tale of youthful fury and savvy overcoming the quicksand of abject poverty and the quaking caste system of India—though this social equation could take place just as well in Detroit or Amsterdam or Cairo. We agreed with the *Washington Post's* assertion that "this outsize celebration of perseverance and moral triumph contains within it a deeper idea—in this case, the relative nature of what we think we know, and what's worth knowing at all." Great music—that reverberated throughout the house all week, whether any of our kids, from 13 to 28, was turning on the switch!

The Reader, with its haunting grayish canvas of postwar and contemporary Germany, and that nation's complex soul-searching process to adjudicate and bury the hideous reality of the extermination of Europe's Jews, crystallized the story into the dark interaction between a vulnerable young man and an emotionless woman. I remember reading Bernhard Schlink's novel long ago; the movie is a gripping realization of sexual obsession (and manipulation) and hard-fought ethical decisions set against the ongoing courtroom struggle of modern Germany to settle the nation's ghoulish legacy—a labyrinth of jurisprudence and shadowy human nature.

Frost/Nixon made me relive the tawdry, repulsive unraveling of the American presidency that came with Richard M. Nixon in the 1970s. I was surprised to see so many younger people in the audience and then realized that they generally equate the presidency with duplicity and televised gimmickry. We agreed with *The Onion's* summary that "Frank Langella highlights Nixon's oily charm and guile." Oh, for a sequel in a few years, President Obama, which celebrates ethical integrity and ethical courage in Washington!

Milk, besides grabbing one's heart, sight, and conscience, is a quickening movie of brilliant colors, moral outrage, and political disturbance. Roger Ebert of the *Chicago Sun-Times* nailed the core of the production: "Sean Penn never tries to show Harvey Milk as a hero, and never needs to. He shows him as an ordinary man, kind, funny, flawed, shrewd, idealistic, yearning for a better world." This is not ultimately a drama of the gay community; it is an American story casting harsh light all the way from "the Castro" in San Francisco into every street, school, and city hall in this country.

Doubt, aside from the entrancing performance of Meryl Streep as an unwavering Catholic school nun and principal who doubts the morals of her easy-going and warm-blooded rector and superior, was better realized on the stage. Philip Seymour Hoffman, a charismatic and intensely fluid actor, was nonetheless miscast in the latter role. We wanted the suspected priest to anguish more visibly with his possible sexual guilt and its ramifications and to dispense with things less handily than with brief chapel homilies more suited to a Hollywood set than a gritty, windy, Queens neighborhood in 1964.

The Boy in the Striped Pajamas should be viewed by every youngster in this country over the age of 9—it is just about the only Holocaust movie ever made that will teach a child about good and evil and innocence and *what happened* without gratuitously relying on the graphic images required for adults. The simplicity of this tale of devastatingly pure friendship between two boys on opposite sides of history's barbed-wire fence is enough to turn your soul inside and out—a good thing. We cannot stop thinking about this little, searing narrative of men's darkest motivations and children's last stand.

Grateful we are that there are cinematic possibilities for making the soul wince.

So you want to use the Bible on the question of Gaza?

January 3, 2009

A well-respected humanitarian, with real travel and work credentials as a peace volunteer and relief specialist, offered a well-meaning statement this week in a major California newspaper. Decrying the bloodshed in Gaza (as if this were the first time), the writer referenced the hallmark incident in the book of Genesis: God, reviling the abhorrent and sadistic behavior of Sodom and Gomorrah, vows to destroy the evil twin cities. Abraham argues with God: "If there are but 50 good people there, will you spare the cities?" God agrees. Our contemporary columnist asserts that there must be at least 50 good people in Gaza, so what is Israel doing destroying the entire place?

A potent question that cries for answers, using the same Bible as orientation: The full vignette tells us that Abraham bargained with God, in fact, until the deity agreed to spare the community if there were even just *ten* good people therein. Sadly, there weren't even ten; the biblical decree stood and the contemptible community was vaporized.

I would argue that there are way more than 50 good people in Gaza—hundreds of thousands of fine folks. Nor does the Israeli government seek to destroy Gaza; it seeks to uncover the leaders of the terrorist organization Hamas and eliminate them, just as the United States has been vociferously trying to do with the despots of Al Qaeda and the like. Regrettably, tragically, unforgivably, Hamas leaders, after winning an election giving them the responsibility to govern Gaza, have turned their attention to bombing Israeli towns and holding the 50+ good people in Gaza hostage.

The writer excoriates Israel for the economic and social disparities that do indeed plague the residents of poverty-stricken, undernourished, undereducated Gazans. This is not an issue derived from Genesis, but it is biblical: If Israel (not Hamas) had been freely elected to govern Gaza, then Israel would likely be providing the same kind of schools, recreation facilities, and infrastructure that it does in the Israeli towns and cities that have been bombed by Hamas all these years.

But let's close by going right back to the Bible, to the same book of Genesis. The painful matter of destroying human communities is too often the stuff of Scripture. The first such episode occurs just prior to the Flood: God tells Noah (Genesis, 9:13): "The end of all flesh is come before me; for the earth is filled with violence through them; and, behold, I will destroy them with the earth."

Attention all Biblical critics using the Scripture to make a point: The Hebrew word for "violence," used in this biblical sentence, is "hamas." You can look it up.

Now it's personal: My nephew is fighting in Gaza
January 5, 2009

There's a sweet lad in the Israel Defense Forces who was named for my late father, Zev. Dad was also a soldier for Israel—back in 1948, when the U.N. created the state and the surrounding Arab nations immediately invaded (and were repelled by a ragtag army of Holocaust survivors and native sons and daughters). Now my nephew is fighting terrorism in Gaza, having been transferred from already difficult duty in the troubled biblical town of Hebron in the West Bank.

I recall a happy, carefree time, a couple of years ago at the Western Wall in Jerusalem. Zev, his younger brother, and two sisters visited the sacred site one night along with their parents and me. My brother Sam was expansive during a happy frolic in the city of peace. Sam and his family are currently ensconced in a Tel Aviv hotel while their village of Gan Yavneh, adjacent to Ashdod, is being barraged by Kassam missiles from Hamas killers in Gaza who are incongruously sworn to a 'holy war' against these families and, generally, the singular successful democracy and cultural and scientific center in the Middle East.

For years, we have heard that Israeli soldiers are uncommonly brave because they literally fight in defense of their own back yards, school houses, shopping centers, and community houses. A polled three-quarters majority of the American people now understand this and at this very moment affirm that Israel's operation in Gaza is "justified."

Naturally, I agree, while my heart is hurting for the children on both sides of this horrific turn of events. But I can't offer a logical dissertation to grown men who swear the name of their God on their lips while admonishing their own kids to be suicide bombers and openly declaring that "the annihilation of the Jews…is a splendid blessing."

The fact is that I wish that my nephew Zev didn't have to be so brave. I wish that he could return to his beloved video games, his profoundly peaceful study of Talmudic brainteasers, and to his active adoration of (and frustration with) the Cincinnati Bengals football club. I want him to tap his feet to his MP3, flirt with girls, and be alive and well at his wedding under a canopy that veils no more missiles of massacre.

And I wish the same for every Zev born of a mother on the other side lucky enough to evade the teachers of hate in the name of a God who left the room a long time ago.

Long ago, from my grandmother's porch in Israel
January 6, 2009

I don't remember much about war in Israel. And in my dreams these nights, I am recalling the most peaceful, sweetest days of my life—my brief years of childhood there.

I remember the orange trees, the thick breezes, my friends who had come home to Israel from all over the world, and my grandmother.

I remember feeling warm and special, talking to her for hours on end, on her porch on the second floor of the apartment building she owned at the corner of Weizmann and Jerusalem Streets in a little town called Kfar-Saba, which means "Village of the Grandfathers."

I remember that the town was founded in 1903 by some farmers who were looking for a new place to grow some grapefruit trees, a few miles west of another, larger town called Petach-Tikva. They found good soil where Kfar-Saba grew up, just a mile or two from the Samarian Mountains and next to an Arab hamlet called Qalqilya.

One of the farmers who planted the grapefruit trees was my grandfather, who was married to my grandmother, but died even before I was born.

Her name was "Yona," which means "the dove," and she came to the land of Israel from Rumania when she was three years old. She had a thin nose, long gray and white braided hair, and wore heavy-laced shoes. She was short but sturdy. Her wrinkles ran together across her cheeks and forehead and around her clear blue eyes and looked like the Hebrew calligraphy on a sheaf of the Torah scroll.

Yona kept all of our family pictures under a glass that fit perfectly over the dining room table. If there wasn't a tablecloth, I would eat my lunch of vegetable meatballs, cucumber and tomato salad, chickpeas, olives, pita bread, and hot tea while staring down at grayish photographs of my departed grandfather, my parents, my cousins, my uncles, aunts, and other people—some of whom were riding on camels and others who wore army shorts, pullover sweaters, and helmets.

I remember the postman who came on a high horse, beaming and proud—especially when there was that rare and prized letter from *America*. He had a tattoo of numbers on his forearm, from his years in Auschwitz. But now he was smiling, the sun beaming down from behind his leathery face and official cap. I remember the bookseller in the village square where we acquired our school texts; he also with the numbers on his arm, reaching across to hand me an arithmetic book written in Hebrew: "Our language is not dead anymore," he would say, a tear in his eyes. "And neither are we."

And then I wake up and realize that Israel is not young anymore, that even the tattooed numbers have given way to time and bitterness and that I'm one of the lucky children from the Middle East who even has dreams.

'Am I my brother's keeper?' is not so applicable to Palestinians

January 7, 2009

The Arab world, proud and complex, has given the world numerology, exotic literature and poetry, rhythmic music, savory cuisine, and a pioneering relationship with the desert. While about 9% of Arabs are Christians, and the belief system is hardly monolithic, the Arab culture is certainly synonymous with Islam, even as we westerners began a crash course in Islamic philosophy on September 11, 2001.

While Cain's infamous rejoinder to God after he slew his brother Abel, "Am I my brother's keeper?" is found in the Old Testament, something with its motif must surely exist in the Koran. Here is the original plea for social justice—particularly as it applies to one's own family, tribe, or creed.

Being from and for Israel should not qualify one's bewilderment at the general abandonment of the Palestinians by the international community—beyond the rhetoric, the cynical use of refugee children (publicly confessed as early as 1961 by King Hussein of Jordan) for political advantage, the outright co-opting of a people's predicament to sell oil and accumulate power for decades now. Just listen to NPR daily or read serious publications and you will hear and see these sad charges made by desperately scorned folks who live in Gaza, Jenin, Ramallah, and elsewhere.

They, the Palestinians themselves, are tired of Egyptian president Hosni Mubarak's manipulation of the situation, the crocodile tears of Syrians and Saudis, the completely disingenuous use of "our Palestinian brothers" by the Al Qaeda syndicate. They are openly disgusted with the corruption, economic and social, of the late Yasir Arafat's Palestinian Authority—an impotent, corpulent band of hypocrites that sit by in the West Bank, having been brutally removed from Gaza by the terrorist agency Hamas and yet claim to represent Palestinian interests.

When the United Nations partitioned Great Britain's Palestine mandate in 1947 into two states, one Jewish and one Arab, the Jewish Agency and the fledgling state of Israel began the first of several sweeping rescue efforts. Jewish refugees—stateless, emaciated—were brought home to Israel from Europe's death camps, from Yemen, Ethiopia, Iraq, Syria, the Soviet Union, and a myriad of other places. The Arab world, by contrast, immediately destroyed any hopes for the indigenous Arabs of Palestine by summarily invading the new Israel—and being trumped.

This morning, the only "humanitarian aid corridor" open to the people of Gaza has been established—by Israel. Like every other morning for over 60 years, life goes on in Jordan, Kuwait, Sudan, Saudi Arabia, Bahrain, etc. Shiite and Sunni bloodbaths continue. Illiteracy reeks. Women remain largely veiled and subjugated. Oh yeah—the Palestinians; we fight in their name. And drive the Jews into the sea.

Am I my brother's keeper?

The seven reasons God isn't talking to us

January 8, 2009

When asked about divine or messianic revelations, most people I speak to boast low expectations. They genuinely believe in God and they may even ardently await a Redeemer. They have a fairly strong engagement with Scripture and essentially take it on faith that God was doing a lot of talking in the biblical stories. But they agree: God has been quiet for a long time, and folks often enough add: "Wouldn't *this* be a good time?"

Contemplating this conundrum, here are 7 possible reasons God isn't taking to us. (Oh: Although I am a genuine advocate of gender-neutral language in liturgy, I will simply fall back on the traditional "he" when referring to the Almighty. It's just a question of form; people will likely chortle if "she" is used, though it is legitimate. Also don't discern much value—or lyricism—when reverting to the "he/ she" format when discussing God.)

God is not talking to us because:

* He's on assignment in another universe and, remember, we invented the clock, not God.

"For a thousand years in your sight are like yesterday when it is past."— (Psalm 90)

* He promised not to destroy the earth again after the Flood. Better he shouldn't open his mouth again since the Flood was due to incredibly egregious human behavior in the first place.

* He can't find us due to ozone layer issues.

* He can't get to us due to all the rocket and satellite space garbage cluttering the firmament.

* He's not sure which theology through which to vent his spleen since he gave us one world and we've answered with several thousand denominational variations, genocidal service gatherings, sundry curses, elitist mantras, and very poor performance.

* He's not in the mood. Again, we're talking God-time; this could be a long delay.

* He *is* talking but we're just not listening, or making too much noise to hear.

Please send in your reasons or comments, even as we pray together for God's closeness.

Weighing in on Oprah
January 9, 2009

Oprah Winfrey's first name is actually a spelling mistake made by a birthing nurse in deep Mississippi in 1954. The child, born into abject poverty and a dysfunctional family situation, was named for the biblical character, Orpah—sister-in-law of Ruth, the consummate convert to Judaism, and a maternal ancestor, according to Christianity, of Jesus. But our Oprah, the ultimate American media icon and true philanthropist, the racial precursor of Barack Obama, is perfectly suited to be herself—even if her name, her credo, her soul don't line up in letters.

This past week, in yet another stirring and admirable personal drama, Ms. Winfrey went very public with her latest weight gain. She even authorized a cover photo for her magazine, *O*, showing the currently 200+ pound Oprah gazing painfully at her earlier svelte and flat-stomached self from several years ago. She has made several printed, Internet, and televised statements decrying her failure and vowing to return to her slimmer self.

There is no more pervasive and spiritually challenging struggle in American life, our vanities and narcissism notwithstanding, than the struggle that so many of us—particularly women—are constantly afflicted with than our weight and physical appearance. This is not to say that there aren't an extraordinary number of fat men in the US. It is to say that men are not held to the excruciating, even callous standards that the media, the fashion world, food industry, the gossip culture, and, yes, *men* impose on women. Men can indulge and look like roly-poly caricatures, and—their metabolic and cardiovascular systems aside—still not be humiliated at work, in a store, or even on television.

In making her confessional so public and bold (a continuing tradition that speaks to Oprah Winfrey's disarming honesty and self-revelation), this remarkable woman has again proven that she is one of the most spiritually centered and mentally healthy women or men in this country.

Oprah Winfrey, the child of unmarried and reckless parents, rose from destitution and a tormented youth to become the most powerful and influential woman in television and, according to *Forbes* magazine, the world's most highly paid entertainer. Though primarily recognized as a talk show hostess, Winfrey also produces and occasionally acts in television movies and feature films that are invariably value-redemptive. But her greatest wealth is the moral currency she brings to the American social scene—with her candor, convictions, and unrelenting commitment to self-improvement. Even as she glitters, we still see the vulnerable and abused child from Mississippi who overcame exploitation, racism, stereotyping in terms of skin color and body shape, and is now our *de facto* cultural prime minister.

In an America brimming dangerously with anorexia, teenage suicide, blatant chauvinism, a saturation of anti-depressants, a sea of vanity, and viral greed, Oprah Winfrey has never been afraid to name symptoms and advocate cures. This standard she has now again applied objectively to herself and I say, God bless her.

My 'things-to-do list,' now that I've been impeached

January 10, 2009

Author's note: *Just got off the phone with Gov. Rod Blagojevich; was wondering if he could appoint me Chief Rabbi of Illinois. Not a problem—I will put check in mail first thing. Asked him about his spiritual outlook, given the 114-1 vote to impeach him in the Illinois state legislature. Inquired if he thought he was a good role model for kids. He replied (I have to say, a little testily): "Hey, I was out jogging when they impeached me. Isn't that a great example? No matter how tough things get, and how many people are on your case, you stay in good shape."*

Governor B. also told me (for additional 3 G's) that he's in great mental condition and was just completing his things-to-do list:

* Tell wife and kids not to worry; Clinton was impeached as president and look at his speaker's fees now.

* Go find 3 more Negroes to appoint to open positions in state and federal governments; these will be post-impeachment courtesy specials.

* Get self on "The View" and cry.

* Go into South Side, have it filmed, and say you were in Baghdad for fact-finding mission.

* Annex Gary, Indiana once and for all then sell it back.

* Get "the guys" to swipe all of Milwaukee's road salt and then announce amazing surplus of same exactly when next blizzard hits Chicago.

* Tell wife and kids not to worry; Clinton was impeached and he can get into any show or party he wants.

* Go to Springfield, give speech reminding people that Lincoln had some strengths, but was inclined to depression and never jogged.

* Ask Treasury Department to bail out Chicago Cubs and then bid off all the private loges. Oh: Have "the guys" knock out those field lights at Wrigley Field and restore nostalgia for old Wrigley. Sell lights to Palin for quick Alaska winter pay-off.

* ~~Get a haircut.~~

No, I am not a Mossad agent, but I did once skip the fare on a bus in Rome

January 12, 2009

An unfriendly reader conveyed a message that since I have been writing so much about the Gaza tragedy, and from the Israeli point of view (as if there is a "point of view" when young people are forced to kill and little children are caught in the middle) that I must be "some kind of Mossad agent." Mossad is Israel's renowned covert agency and they must be so good that I don't even know I'm on their payroll.

Another misanthrope, seeing in war yet another opportunity to safely grandstand from the safety of his suburban laptop, wondered why I don't mind my own business and "stick to spirituality." As though war is not the most malignant spiritual disaster; what shall we do about it but post some more pious platitudes? Like Martin Luther King, Jr. (to whom I adamantly do not compare myself) who stood up one year before his death in a church and decried the Vietnam War—against the advice of his allies and with the excoriation of his enemies—we who labor for God must speak up when the human spirit is co-opted by terrorists and draconian "leaders."

The misconceptions about Israel's painstaking operation to stop terrorist missile attacks upon its towns and villages from Hamas operatives in Gaza are not as great as I might have thought. It may seem a trite configuration, but a whopping 78% of those polled on America Online still regard it as "justified." AOL is hardly a Jewish web site; the Jews, meanwhile, represent less than 2% of the US population. The US Senate has unanimously voted in support of the operation. A number of evangelical organizations, so outspoken in their admiration for and veneration of the Jewish state, have registered their encouragement. Everyone who gets it, who understands that finding Hamas gangsters is the equivalent of America's search for Al Qaeda operatives, is profoundly saddened by the loss of innocent lives.

And yet: Here is what Ralph Peters, a career intelligence officer, and a veteran analyst and columnist , wrote yesterday in the *New York Post*:

> *"Israel hasn't killed a single civilian in the Gaza Strip.(Hundreds of) civilians have died, and Israeli bombs or shells may have ended their lives. But Israel didn't kill them.*
>
> *"Hamas did. It's time to smash the lies. The lies of Hamas. The UN lies. And the save-the-terrorists lies of the global media.*
>
> *"There is no moral equivalence between Hamas terrorists and Israeli soldiers. There is no gray area. There is no point in negotiations.*
>
> *"Hamas is a Jew-killing machine. It exists to destroy Israel. What is there to negotiate?*
>
> *"When Hamas can't kill Jews, it's perfectly willing to drive Palestinian civilians into the line of fire—old men, women and children. Hamas herds the innocent into "shelters," then draws Israeli fire on them. And the headline-greedy media cheer them on.*
>
> *"All Hamas had to do to prevent Israel's act of self-defense was to leave Israel unmolested by terror rockets. All Hamas needs to do now to stop this conflict and spare the Palestinian people it pretends to champion is to stop trying to kill Israelis and agree to let Israel exist in peace.*
>
> *Hamas didn't, and Hamas won't."*

As for me, I'm sorry I rode the bus for free from Via Veneto to Piazza Navone that time, but at least I'm owning up to it.

'Hi, I'm Mike King and, sorry, I have a cold'

January 13, 2009

As a student and teacher of the mind of Dr. Martin Luther King, Jr., one becomes sentimental every January—the month of his birth and an annual, mercantile-free (so far) interval of reflection and social service seminars. Martin would have turned 80 this Thursday. But not only that: Martin Luther King Day, Monday, January 19, falls 24 hours prior to the inauguration of Barack Obama as the 44th president of the United States. The Obama family has linked the two days with a "Renew America Day" of volunteerism and good works.

I have a lifelong obsession with finding people who actually interacted with the man born as "Mike" on January 15, 1929. There was Dr. Joan Campbell, the one-time General Secretary of the National Council of Churches, who related a story to me about M.L. King while we both appeared on a Cleveland podium for an MLK Day Convocation several years ago.

"We were expecting him one afternoon for a dedication ceremony of some kind. This was in the mid-sixties. My doorbell rang at home. Outside in the rain stood a rather small young man, alone in a raincoat. He said, 'Hi, I'm Mike King.' He apologized profusely because he had a cold. He needed some attention and I warmed him up with some soup and some cough medicine. He was just so humble."

This scene, having taken place in a Shaker Heights, Ohio home—in the same community where my two daughters grew up—has never left me. The humanity of it, and the tenderness of it, makes me swell up with curiosity and envy. How I would have liked to have given Mike King something warm to eat, and to just chat with him about the rain, children, life itself! This recollection of Dr. Campbell: How it stands in juxtaposition to the untold times that Dr. King was subjected to blows, insults, expulsions, and the cold soup of prison.

My longtime friend, Congressman Louis Stokes, one-time chairman of the Congressional Black Caucus as well as the House Investigation Committee on Assassinations, remembers a telling moment with Martin Luther King. Louis' brother, Carl, was elected mayor of Cleveland in November,

1967—Carl was the first African-American to ever be elected mayor of a major American city. (Ironically, I was a co-officiant at Carl Stokes' funeral in 1996; Jesse Jackson spoke the eulogy).

Dr. King was in Cleveland for the tight balloting and shared an upstairs conference room with the Stokes brothers in a downtown building on election night. When word came that Carl had narrowly won the mayoralty, he had to go downstairs to meet the press and accept the results. According to Louis Stokes, Carl invited Dr. King to join him at the podium. King politely declined, saying: "If I go down there with you, people will be looking at me and this should be all about you." Brother Louis was not comfortable just leaving MLK by himself so he spent a long interval chatting privately with King in the room while Carl went down to accept the historic election outcome. The Talmud says: 'He who does not exalt himself will be exalted by Heaven."

Pres. Bush's 'Twelve things-to-do-list' before leaving office
January 13, 2009

Author's note: *When I had the pleasure of meeting the president a few years ago, he reassured me and the other rabbis present that "As a Christian, I pray for Israel's survival every day. As an American, I know better." This Talmudic logic has never stopped hurting my head. I hope to figure out what the man from Crawford was talking about while life is still inside of me.*

Meanwhile, using the same logic, the Dept. of Spiritual Life has devised the 43rd president's "12 Things-to-do-list" before leaving office:

* Find the guy that put up that **'Mission Accomplished'** banner.
* Learn a mind trick to make me not chortle every time I run into **McCain.**
* See how **the Israelis** are keeping that old Gen. Sharon alive all these years and get some of that stuff.
* Try hard not to yell "Ha, ha, you voted for Buchanan" when I get the big speaking engagements at any of those **Jewish** old ladies' gatherings in Florida.
* Give Poppy Bush Jeb's **cell phone** number and tell him it's mine.
* See when Bud Selig is finally going to retire as **baseball** commissioner—that's my job for God's sake. No foreign policy and everybody has to buy a seat.
* Ask Poppy once and for all how it is that **Texas** is part of Connecticut.
* Get up to **Alaska** and see what the deal is for myself.
* ~~Get up enough nerve to ask Cheney where he actually lived all these 8 years.~~
* Get to work on my memoirs, *Never Misunderestimate Me,* and make sure it gets on all the Internets.
* Remember to call **Obama** once a month and tell him "I know I left you between Iraq and a hard place yuk yuk."
* Take a course on the Google about weather patterns outside Texas.

Bush's 'I don't know' on Bin Laden is final moral abdication
January 14, 2009

Was he kidding? Sitting smugly across from Larry King during an exit interview, dutiful wife Laura alongside, bobbing her head, President Bush answered the talk show host's question:

"Were we ever close to capturing Osama Bin Laden?"

"Oh, I don't know," shrugged the 43rd president of the United States, who has defined his presidency by that very capture, who feels "called" by heaven to have presided over this nation of ours exactly at the outbreak on "The War on Terror," who swaggered aimlessly through history and deceit in the aftermath of America's greatest opportunity to rally the world behind us after the unspeakable events of 9/11.

I don't know? CNN analyst Hillary Rosen, wise and delightfully unglamorous, an actual thinker, described it as "shocking"—even the veil of television could not hide her genuine incredulity at such glibness.

This is not a political disaster (well, actually it is). This is a final moral abdication in front of the American people—an upbeat people who have borne under this administration's calcified relationship with principles, morals, and the dispensing of young lives in favor of self-serving and jingoistic policies.

I don't know? First of all, doesn't he himself discern how such a dismissal completely dismantles any hope he has of historical integrity and a legacy that isn't laughable? But OK, so he doesn't seem to be in touch with his own soul and thereby his own term as leader of the free world. Why bring the whole presidency down with him? Isn't the president *supposed* to know about things like that?

Here's what he *did* know last night on CNN: That the government's response to Katrina was actually "pretty good" because don't you recall that "we picked up 30,000 people off of roofs?" Never mind that the city of New Orleans was left completely abandoned and drowning on the ground and that the tragedy reopened old racial wounds that may now heal again, thank goodness. Oh, W, if only you'd had come down off the roof while you squandered your presidency, our men and women in uniform, our prestige, our economy, our self-confidence, our economy, our good spirits!

President Bush did know definitively about one thing: He will not become Commissioner of Baseball upon the retirement of Bud Selig. At least we know that home is safe in that sense.

Wonder what John McCain is doing this weekend

January 16, 2009

Forgive me, but I'm not the only one who had trouble discerning who exactly John McCain was while running for the White House this fall against our now imminent president Barack Obama. The press frequently reported that even members of his own Republican Party didn't know what to make of him, weren't "comfortable" with him, or just avoided him. Meanwhile, he shunned George W. Bush much of the time, he resisted being the same person he was in 2000, he avoided smiling a lot except when he appeared to also have a porcupine stuck in his collar, he eluded David Letterman, and he generally avoided being an attractive national candidate.

This is a question of looking into a man's soul.

McCain, a sudden sycophant of spiritual tyrants, cavorted with a number of people, non-inclusive right-wing preachers in particular, and others who patronize women and their right to make their own decisions about life and love and the future. This was after he had spent a long portion of his career advocating for progressivism and compassion—or at least pragmatism—in such matters of the human condition. The "maverick" sold his soul to the radicalized base and he looked like it. There was a false face to him, a sense of inner doom. He even admitted to television host Jon Stewart that, yes, he'd "gone over to the other side." He was better than that stranger who possessed his electoral body.

His choice of a running mate, cynical, condescending, ill-conceived, and regrettable, made everything else for which he thrust away his conscience seem Palin comparison.

McCain, who really did suffer, and for a very long time, as a prisoner of the North Vietnamese after being shot down over Hanoi, nonetheless became the third consecutive Vietnam veteran to lose the presidential election to someone who never saw active duty in the US military. That's an achievement for a hearty Washington veteran with an independent streak who is authentically decorated and without question loves America and would have appeared to be an ideal national candidate.

John McCain seemed liberated, even relieved, as the rigorous election marathon wound down and it was clear that the younger, calmer, non-impulsive, non-jingoistic, oratorical, patient, consensus-building, in-tune, sincere Barack Obama was going not only to win—but to finally blur the distinction between red and blue, black and white, patriot and activist.

Sen. John McCain, who is a man of tremendous insight and uncommon experiences, forgot to just be himself in the 2008 campaign. Barack Obama never was anything but himself. We Americans are a good people who were simply looking for a thoughtful leader that was improving, not improvising. It came down to both men's inner souls, and, thankfully, not their skin.

Courtney Love not showing love for her Jewish parts
January 17, 2009

Courtney Love of San Francisco, Ireland, New Zealand, Liverpool, Minneapolis, Portland, OR, and a variety of other places induced by LSD, has apparently sworn off her Jewish descent. The one-time band organizer, Mickey Mouse Club-reject, stripper, and frequent litigant was married to rock star Kurt Cobain for two years until his heroin-induced suicide in 1994. She is the mother of their child, Frances Bean Cobain, a youngster being raised, well, in an alternative world of new wave values and punk anger—much as Courtney was raised by her own mother.

It is impossible to know how this tragically talented young woman and counter-cultural specialist could possibly cohere spiritually, given her life experience of social volatility, drug carnivals, including alleged LSD use introduced by her father when she was three, sexual escapades that began before she was a teen, and the global vagabonding of her thrice-divorced mother—with whom she was stuck, driven, abandoned, picked up, and generally embroiled.

Unfortunately for the house of Israel, Courtney had a Jewish grandmother, a novelist, whom she didn't like. It follows that every pejorative she can associate with Jewish people, agencies, or institutions flow out of her like grunge.

In the category of the soul, Ms. Love is homeless. Her heritage—rhythmic, creative, wild—is biologically Irish-Jewish-Cuban. For whatever reason, from the midst of her internal whirlwind, she has decided to spring forth wrath, self-contempt, and expletives on her Jewish loins. Oy, such a meltdown: Courtney, who is as rich as she is racist, nonethless has no use for Jewish stereotypes.

Quoted in *Heeb* Magazine and then at least two major New York newspapers, Love declared: "Every time you buy a Nirvana record, part of that money is *not* going to Kurt's child, or to me, it's going to a handful of Jew loan officers, Jew private banks." It should be noted that this impossibly controversial singer and songwriter has also been so sparing of other clusters of humanity, including animal rights activists: "Yep, I'm a fur whore. If it's 100 years old, I'm f—king into it. Sorry PETA. I've been very, very good for a very, very long time, and this ermine is ancient and tattered and feels like it belonged to a Queen. I know, I know. Maybe I'll just stare at it, but f--off if I wear it, I KNOW what I'm doing." Thus she blogged, setting an example for young text messengers as numerous as the stars.

In the end, I'm not worried about Courtney Love's anti-Semitism or the fact that she mocks all her roots by calling herself a "Jew-ban." I'm certainly not concerned about her bank accounts or her access to the press. I'm worried about Courtney herself, and a young woman named Frances Bean—who may have every possession imaginable but remains woefully impoverished. Here's my hope that somebody—Cuban, Irish, Jewish, whatever—intervenes and helps Courtney realize something. Love is not just a name.

Blue eyes, a lot of love, and then a dreadful accident

January 18, 2009

He was tall, though not gangly, soft-spoken, and exceedingly handsome. When I first met Marty, already well into his eighties, I was so struck by his fitness, his quiet elegance, and above all, those deep blue eyes. Though I saw some sadness in those eyes, and certainly a lot of experience, they still glistened, like Mediterranean pools, every time he approached. He was also smiling and extending a warm hand of welcome.

Marty was actually part of the little search tribunal that engaged me as rabbi of an unusual and priceless congregation of elders here in Southern California. It's a part-time position around which I build a variety of creative pursuits but it's a full-time love affair (certainly for me). Marty was but one of a host of venerable human beings who endow me, week after week on Friday evenings, with their knowledge, their love of life, their courage, their sorrows, their regrets, their triumphs, their prayers, and their bittersweet wisdom.

They have virtually all come to the community and built a congregation from many different places; Marty was from Connecticut. He spoke to me more often with that generous grin and his ritualistic and firm handshake than with chatter. He never had the need to tell me too much and I don't know (now to my regret) if he knew how much I *depended* upon our weekly handshake and greeting as a kind of private bellwether.

There was an occasion when we spoke, both making our way from the service to the auxiliary hall where the two hundred or so weekly attendees share some coffee, tea, cake, and conversation. As things are, the discussion among such congregants and their rabbi is not infrequently about illness, mortality, or death itself. It is a lively group, astonishingly active, filled with music, theater, books, and travel. The adult community (which includes a number of faith societies and a bevy of social clubs, athletic centers, and a verdant golf course set against the mountains) is still a retirement city after all. I was sharing with Marty my deep sadness about a member of our congregation who had lost an adult child.

In the only instance during which Marty spoke at any length about himself, he looked at me, perfectly erect and without any drama, and said: "Someday I'll tell you, Rabbi. I lost both of my children."

Someday never came. Marty had also buried a wife of many years, though he enjoyed a delicate love affair for some five years there in the community with an exquisite woman who also knows from widowhood. Leaving a Brotherhood meeting last Sunday over which he presided with his hallmark cheerfulness and dignity, Marty drove away, suffered a massive coronary and died as his car flipped over.

It is our clinging hope that Marty was gone before the vehicle coiled.

Only in the aftermath, as I came to officiate at the burial and memorial of a man I honestly loved, did I learn the extent of his blue-eyed goodness. He dedicated his life to an agency that gives hope to mentally challenged kids—like his departed son. The losses, as well, of his daughter and his wife only conveyed to Marty what this life actually means and requires of us. But Marty, why did you leave before I got to hear you tell the story yourself?

MARTIN LUTHER KING DAY
JANUARY 19, 2009

INAUGURATION OF PRESIDENT

BARACK H. OBAMA

JANUARY 20, 2009

'White /Colored' was posted and I will never forget
January 19, 2009

On this most historic MLK Day, my thoughts drift to a very hot day near Lake City, Florida, August 1963—the same month in which Rev. King would deliver his enduring "I Have A Dream" oration in Washington, DC.

My father, mother, my younger brother and I had set out from Cincinnati in my father's prized ivory-white '57 Chevy Impala and taken one of our family trips, this time to Miami Beach. My immigrant dad adored the American countryside and knew of no other travel possibility than of the highways, official state maps, Stuckey's pecan pies and any good local hamburger place, along with clean, if basic, motels that featured well-stocked ice machines and fresh Coca-Colas. My father, a stocky, looming man who was a minor soccer legend and decorated war veteran back in our native Israel, always remained socially progressive. "Kennedy" was a magical name in our household; my father's singular political achievement was being elected as a delegate to the 1972 Democratic Convention on a slate committed to Senator Henry "Scoop" Jackson.

On a smoldering day in August, 1963, we pulled into a filling station, the Chevrolet kicking up bone-dry gravel and dirt into the Florida sky. The Marchers for Jobs and Freedom were preparing to convene in Washington; President John F. Kennedy (who initially opposed the march) had two months left to live. Near Lake City, my father and I stepped out of our car to wash up while an attendant pumped gasoline into the vehicle and wiped the windshield.

In the dust we created, we hadn't noticed a second car that pulled up at the same time. Another father and son, black, were also making their way towards the restrooms. The lad was more or less my age. I wondered which pair of us would get into the toilet first, but it didn't matter. They were headed for the one marked COLORED, off to the right a bit. The door was rotting with grime; the facility had none of the outside glow and finish and sparkle of our WHITE gateway on the left. Shoes crunching on the gravel, the four of us, two worlds, briefly crossed in the path. I noticed that the other father looked down and that his shoulders resigned into his overall straps; the intense sun blocked me from seeing my father's face.

But my eyes and those of my counterpart's met directly for a brief instant. I looked into something hollow, anonymous, but strangely defiant. He was not ashamed, or maybe he didn't know to be ashamed, which is what I hoped for in that pubescent intersection of ancient rites and evil laws.

My father and I did our business and he was uncharacteristically silent, which told me everything. When we drove away moments later, I looked into the other family's Rambler station wagon but, again, the western Florida sun blinded me and everything else on the earth.

Today we can see again.

Were they owed this?

January 21, 2009

Somebody asked me this recently and I continue to assume that it was not a leading question, and that it was part of an honest intellectual exercise. The remarkable dimensions of Barack Obama's ascent to the American presidency—which was matched by the quiet grandeur of his inaugural ceremonies yesterday—invoke or provoke a layer of reactions. We think about it in historical terms, in the context of race, and within the configurations of the natural, prevailing American proclivity towards self-improvement.

But were they owed this; *they* meaning America's black community? Did electing Barack Obama somehow offer a cathartic path for our subconscious guilt over not only slavery and segregation, but our individual submersions into racism? Please no! If this was why the brilliant, composed, deliberate young man who was sworn into office yesterday, and intoned a 21st century political homily that was based entirely upon inclusion as well as the general welfare of all Americans, then we are more racist than ever and his astonishing and inspirational victory is a sham.

Dr. Martin Luther King, Jr. would have been downcast if he were still alive, only to arrive at the desultory conclusion that the president arrived to salve our national conscience. He would have felt patronized and betrayed—the Reverend pleaded with us to choose people precisely *not* because of skin color. No, this was not a matter of national affirmative action even as black folks (and white folks, too) wept with the hagiographic feel of it. No matter what, it must be hard for older black folks who were personally shoved to the rear of busses, who were routinely called dreadful names, who systemically were excluded from good schools, fresh water, and the protection of police, not to have been emotionally overwhelmed when they actually saw their icon assume the highest office in the land and in human chronicles.

But "they" were not owed this. No decent and responsible citizen of any color or creed would ever arbitrate American executive power over the posterity of grievance. "They" were owed the advantage of the Emancipation Proclamation from 1863, not the heartbreaking upshot of Reconstruction and Jim Crow laws that were not even negotiated until 1963. "They" were owed jobs, text books, and decent wages. Nobody owed them the presidency. "They" were just entitled to compete for it like anybody else. "They" were owed the release of not being "they" anymore.

We were all owed this: A new beginning, a sense of hope, a relief from the despondency that had penetrated the marrow of American life. It just turns out that a young man of Kenyan descent and global wisdom and Chicago savvy made us feel very happy yesterday—an unseasonably sunny and glorious day in the federal village named for a founding president who, incidentally, owned slaves.

The long and bittersweet journey of Ted Kennedy

January 22, 2009

When President and Mrs. Obama went to pray yesterday morning at Washington's National Cathedral, one recalled another occasion at such a vaunted church.

It was June, 1968, and a thin, square-jawed, broken-hearted man spoke of his murdered brother: It was Senator Edward M. Kennedy at New York's St. Patrick's Cathedral, trembling with grief and eloquence, eulogizing his brother Robert—who had been gunned down at the Ambassador Hotel in Los Angeles after having just won the California Democratic presidential primary.

If you are old enough to remember certain things as they happened, then you remember Ted Kennedy's distinct voice cracking with anguish when he declared that "Love is not an easy feeling to put into words."

Ted Kennedy, the lion-hearted liberal, the most beloved and despised member of Congress over a sustained and unwavering legislative reign in Washington of some four decades, is certainly the only member of the Senate with this harsh badge: All three of his older brothers died young and violently. Joe, an army pilot, was shot down over Europe in World War II; John, the president, was assassinated in Dallas on Nov. 22, 1963; Bobby, clearly en route to the presidency, was murdered on June 5, 1968.

There have always been questions about this surviving young brother, Ted, now 76, afflicted with terminal brain cancer, who survived a plane crash in 1965 that broke his back, endured tragedies that rival Greek mythology, overcame the legacy of his rather shady, bigoted, and indulgent father, Joseph Kennedy, Sr., and who nonetheless will always have the shadow of Chappaquiddick over him. In 1969, Ted Kennedy drove off Dike Bridge near Chappaquiddick Island and into Poucha Pond. He swam to safety but his passenger, a young woman named Mary Jo Kopechne, drowned. Kennedy did not report the incident until the next day; his eventual suspended sentence and the suspicious death of Kopechne will ever haunt history.

But about this there is no question: No figure in contemporary chronicles has ever held public office and stubbornly produced an uninterrupted body of social legislation (that actually dwarfs the legislative achievements of any president since FDR) while carrying the unyielding grief of having lost iconic brothers to successive assassinations. It is impossible to imagine what this does to a person—even as Sen. Kennedy has been a surrogate father to a great circle of nieces and nephews and, as such, has even buried children in the extended Kennedy family. When he ran for president in 1980 and lost the primary battle to President Jimmy Carter, it was clear that Ted Kennedy didn't even really want it—he is the most threatened public figure in Washington and has been for over 40 years.

Sen. Kennedy collapsed just after the inauguration the other day of the man he boldly endorsed early in the campaign; today he is recouping again, likely commiserating with his niece Caroline, who has withdrawn from consideration as New York's senator. The Kennedy story wanes, but Ted Kennedy, weathered, real, boisterous, will likely not wane until the eternal rest at last gives him peace.

OK, I'm ready for my bail-out now

January 25, 2009

Dear Secretary of the Treasury-designate Geithner:

I know that you are a little busy presently explaining all your "honest mistakes," and may have one or two things ahead of me in your inbox. But, let's be real, the Senate will confirm you and you have suffered patiently with all the inevitable Republican grandstanding given their shellacking on Election Day. Always good to note the soul-searching on Capitol Hill.

So, given your imminent receipt of the Treasury keys and the current great mood about throwing money around so generously to solve a lot of problems, and given the fact that the former CEO of Merrill Lynch spent $1.2 million to refurbish his office digs and hasn't been tarred and feathered in Herald Square, my sense is you are receptive to curative and PR-savvy good-citizen moves.

Compared to the sums required by some of our hard-boiled and legacy-run banks to "make it," what I need shouldn't be much more than about $590,000. (Trying to keep it reasonable for the sake of patriotism and national service.) I did buy out the lease on my 2004 Audi A6 about a year ago but I've noticed that the driver-side mirror has to be electronically readjusted each time I get in the vehicle—exactly when I'm focused on resetting the bass/treble/fade controls on the 8-speaker audio system. This is really a distraction and I won't even mention that the car has no form of GPS whatsoever. So it's time to think about a hearty keyless-entry Lexus 460 (I hear they assemble a lot of cars in Kentucky) and while I do like the Audi brand, it's time to eschew German equipment after all is said and done.

My stepdaughter, a career Obama girl incidentally, very green and veggie (she insists we stop purchasing spring water in individual bottles and is mercury-obsessed with the oceans) really needs a car herself, now that she's almost 16. But I think a mid-sized GM van would be more in line with her carpool ambitions and—oh—she wants to spend a summer in Spain to finally master the new-wave language challenges of this multi-cultural America and experience summer humidity without the benefit of high-level American air-conditioning. Thought I'd fly her over there and check out some rental property in Barcelona so maybe we're looking at something closer to $850,000 by now.

My oldest daughter, a promising and energetic twenty-something living in Brooklyn and commuting to theater auditions in Manhattan—she insists on using mass transit only—really needs a break from the grind. Given that she was born in Canada and we now have a president with Kenyan roots (great story, incidentally), shouldn't we be sending her out as an exchange cultural emissary to the Russian National Theater? With Putin and whatever-the-president's-name-is blowing a lot of Cold War steam, are not dramaturgy and music the wave of Facebook-era diplomacy? Gosh, this will bring the total to about $1.1 million but it's still less than the guy from Merrill Lynch and his George the IVth desk and mahogany credenza.

Look, if we just round this off to a quick $2 million, I'll pay off our mortgage and not bother you again. It looks like my lending institution is currently three banks in a kinetic merger; let's move quickly and help them, too.

About the Author

Ben Kamin is a rabbi, journalist, author, teacher, community leader, and a specialist in multicultural relations. His Op-ed commentaries have frequently appeared in *The New York Times* and he has been a contributing columnist to the Cleveland *Plain Dealer* and the San Diego *Union Tribune*. He lives in Del Mar, California with his wife, Audrey. When he's not enjoying time with her and the four children they share, Ben is wondering if there ever will be a baseball team again like the 1976 Cincinnati Reds.

Visit Ben's columns at www.examiner.com/www.examiner.com/x-689-
Spiritual-Life-Examiner
Visit Ben at Reconciliation,
"The Synagogue Without Walls"
at
www.benkamin.com